Medicine

UNCOVERED

trotman

Medicine

UNCOVERED

Laurel Alexander

Medicine Uncovered
This first edition published in 2003 by Trotman and Company Ltd
2 The Green, Richmond, Surrey TW9 1PL

© Trotman and Company Limited 2003

Editorial and Publishing Team

Author Laurel Alexander
Editorial Mina Patria, Editorial Director; Rachel Lockhart,
Commissioning Editor; Anya Wilson, Editor; Erin Milliken,
Editorial Assistant.
Production Ken Ruskin, Head of Pre-press and Production
Sales and Marketing Deborah Jones, Head of Sales & Marketing

Designed by XAB

British Library Cataloguing in Publication Data
A catalogue record for this book is available
from the British Library

ISBN 0 85660 897 1

Typeset by Palimpsest Book Production Limited,
Polmont, Stirlingshire

Printed and bound in Great Britain by
Creative Print & Design (Wales) Ltd

CONTENTS

Acknowledgements

I would like to extend my thanks to the NHS, armed forces, professional associations and institutes that kindly furnished me with career information.

CHAPTER 1

What's in it for me?

A career in health isn't something to be sneezed at. The old adage used to be that you had to have a 'vocational calling' to work in the health profession. What this really meant was that you didn't mind a low wage because what you really wanted to do was to 'help' people. However, it's all well and good to want to help others, but you need to put a roof over your head and food in your belly as well. So is it possible to earn a good whack and help others? We hear in the news that nurses, for example, don't earn much. To a certain extent, the salary of a nurse will depend on where you work, e.g. in the private or public sector, in the UK or abroad. In the early stages of post-qualification, salaries are bound to be lower. But as you gain experience and further qualifications, your earnings will undoubtedly rise.

Wannabe an NHS consultant?
Consultants are highly trained senior doctors, many of them working in hospitals. Consultants are normally appointed in their early to mid-30s, having completed at least 15 years of medical training (including 10 years of service in the NHS as

senior house officer and then specialist registrar). The UK has around 26,000 consultants, of whom 20 per cent are women.

After qualifying, consultants earn, as of April 2003, a minimum £63,000. A new contract also puts a 40-hour limit on the basic consultant working week.

So what can NHS consultants earn from private practice? Anything from a small fortune to pocket money, depending on speciality and predisposition. The average net annual private practice income for an NHS plastic surgeon is £75,000 (1999 figures). Orthopaedic surgeons rake in an average of £58,000 a year from private practice. The least lucrative speciality is pathology (£7,572). The very top surgeons can earn upwards of £250,000 on top of their NHS work.

WHAT'S THIS BOOK ABOUT?

If you're reading this book, then you have an interest in health and medicine. But maybe you're not sure about what a career in medicine really means. Maybe you're not sure about the length of training or commitment to study. Maybe you're not sure if the financial rewards are worth the effort you need to put in at the start and throughout your training.

This opening chapter is designed to whet your appetite, to give you an idea of the scope and different environments that medicine works in.

The next chapter offers some gob-smacking facts about medicine. If you choose to embark upon a career in medicine, you are entering a profession that has been around ever since the human condition has existed, roughly 50,000 years!

Chapter 3 moves on to a bit of self-analysis. Have you got what it takes to be a medical practitioner? Which area of medicine might repay further investigation?

Chapter 4 introduces you to the different roles in medicine and the nitty-gritty of how you get into training for these careers.

The last chapter helps you to focus on where you want to go next. Read this chapter for action planning and how to progress your interest.

It's very easy to ignore your feet, especially as they are at the end of your body! That sounds trite, but for a yachtsman sailing over a long period of time, feet problems can affect performance. I went to see my podiatrist, who prescribed an orthosis, which is personalised and numbered on the back; just as well because I couldn't afford to lose it!
Andy Hindley, yachtsman and second in command of Team Philips, Britain's biggest, fastest, most technologically advanced racing yacht

WHAT'S IN IT FOR ME?

You're flicking through this book because you're at a pivotal point in your career choice. What do I want to do? Will I like doing this or that? How much money will I make? Can I do it? It's exciting. But in order to make informed choices, you need to know what medicine is about, whether it's right for you personally and how to move forward in making your dreams of a career in medicine a reality. So, what's in this book for you? Everything you need to plan your next step – even if it's to say, nope, not for me, mate. Or if this book does inspire you, then it's a crucial stepping-stone to job satisfaction and financial reward. You can't lose.

WHERE COULD A CAREER IN MEDICINE TAKE ME?

Still interested in medicine? Did you know you could work in all kinds of different environments? Take for example, the Sikh Community Health Promotion Project. The screening programmes, support groups, exhibitions and written material all needed input from qualified health professionals.

Sikh Community Health Promotion Project (SCHPP)
SCHPP health promotion programmes were run on the radio in Birmingham for a consecutive three years. Over 20 health topics were discussed to create awareness in the Sikh/Punjabi community. Over 80 screening programmes checking physical health have been held in voluntary, public and educational settings. The project has also set up support groups for both genders in Sparkhill and Handsworth. Banners and exhibitions on various health topics have been prepared; and bilingual booklets, posters and leaflets on recipes, diabetes, heart disease, exercise, alcohol, nutrition and other health topics have all been produced and made available to the Sikh community. The project has established firm roots for better health in the community.
Council of Sikh Gurdwaras in Birmingham, 627 Stratford Road South, Birmingham B11 4LS. Tel: 0121 773 0399. Email: info@sikhcouncil.org

Have you considered working abroad with a medical qualification? Suitably qualified health professionals are needed all over the world.

What's it like nursing in Australia?
You'll find it a little different from the UK, although overall it's quite similar. One difference is that registered nurses do most nursing: there are very few enrolled nurses or auxiliaries. Hospitals are generally much newer and more modern than those in Britain and work is available in either in the public system or private hospitals. Posts are graded according to experience. For example, the grading of an RN increases each year, from grade 1 to grade 8. The grading also indicates level of pay.

What's it like nursing in New Zealand?
Working as a nurse in New Zealand is similar to the UK. The conditions in hospitals are good; many have been upgraded in recent years. The hospitals vary in size from small 150-

bed rural hospitals to large 500-bed tertiary care facilities. Most nurses work eight-hour rostered shifts that include night duty. Many hospitals have, or are introducing Clinical Career Pathways. The nurses working on a Career Pathway are paid according to the level they have achieved. Other nurses are paid according to their years of experience.

Worldwide Healthcare Exchange provides health care work, particularly nursing jobs, in Australia and New Zealand. Website: www.whe.co.uk/index.htm

These are some of the different job roles and opportunities in the medical department at Schering Health Care in Sussex:

- Clinical Research Associates: working as part of the European clinical operations organisation. Much of the daily work is with investigators, monitoring clinical trials taking place primarily in the UK, with opportunities to work in Europe.

- Medical Information Scientists: providing an in-depth information service to clinicians and colleagues in marketing and sales.

- Regulatory Affairs: progressing licence applications for new products and licence extensions.

- Biometrics: also working as part of the European clinical operations group, providing either statistical and/or computer programming and maintenance for the valuable data gathered from clinical trials, in preparation for licence applications.

Or what about providing care and rehabilitation to survivors of torture and other forms of organised violence? The Medical Foundation (96–98 Grafton Road, Kentish Town, London NW5 3EJ; website: www.torturecare.org.uk) does just that. They provide survivors of torture in the UK with medical treatment, practical assistance and psychotherapeutic support as well as having a crucial role in educating the public and decision-makers about torture and its consequences and ensuring that Britain honours its international obligations towards survivors of torture, asylum seekers and refugees.

Information is available about current and future skill needs within medicine. The government produces an annual Skills and Labour Market Trends publication, and your nearest Learning and Skills Council (look in your local Yellow Pages) will usually produce an annual assessment of the labour market in your area. In addition to this, you can usually find out about the predicted skill needs within a particular industry/occupation from the professional body/training organisation that represents that industry/occupation. Use this information to inform your career choice and your choice of education/training.

So now you're hooked enough to want to read on. Let's take a visit to the past to see what your future may be based on.

CHAPTER 2

Setting the Scene for Medicine

The medical profession has a rich and varied history spanning centuries and cultures from all around the globe. This chapter isn't written to be a dusty lesson, but to open up a colourful tapestry of how the past has set the scene for medicine today.

THE ROOTS OF MEDICINE

The profession of medicine has a fascinating history.

- Prehistoric skulls found in Europe and South America indicate that Neolithic man was able to trephine (remove disks of bone from the skull) successfully, but whether this delicate operation was performed to release evil spirits or as a surgical procedure is not known.

- Modern medicine owes much to the ancient Egyptians. Such was the extent of Egyptian knowledge that there are records of over 800 medical procedures and remedies making use of over 600 drugs and a vast array of surgical tools.

- In China medicine developed in a unique way. The *Nei Ching*, attributed to the Emperor Huang-Ti, contains a reference to a theory of the circulation of the blood and the function of the heart that suggests familiarity with anatomy. In addition, accurate location of the proper points for the traditional Chinese practice of acupuncture implies some familiarity with the nervous and vascular systems.

- The ancient Hindus seem to have been familiar with many surgical procedures, demonstrating skill in such techniques as nose reconstruction (rhinoplasty) and cutting for removal of bladder stones.

- Medical practice in ancient Greece was based largely upon religious beliefs. The cult of Asclepios, a major provider of medical care, developed old theories and introduced several treatments not too dissimilar from modern complementary medicine. The works of Hippocrates, the father of Western medicine, and his followers led to several scientific facts being recorded for the first time. The work of these philosophers began a tradition of studying the cause of disease rather than looking solely at the symptoms when prescribing a cure. Hippocrates taught the prevention of disease through a regimen of diet and exercise; he emphasised careful observation of the patient, the recuperative powers of nature, and a high standard of ethical conduct, as incorporated in the Hippocratic Oath.

- The Islamic authorities placed great value on medicine. Baghdad had a hospital by AD 850 and by AD 931 doctors had to pass medical examinations in order to practise. Hospitals were later developed throughout the Islamic world, the most famous in Damascus and Cairo.

- By the thirteenth century there were flourishing medical schools at Montpellier, Paris, Bologna and Padua, the latter being the site of production of the first accurate books on human anatomy.

- In the seventeenth century William Harvey demonstrated the circulation of the blood. The introduction of quinine marked a triumph over malaria, one of the oldest plagues of mankind, and the invention of the compound microscope led to the discovery of minute forms of life.

● In the eighteenth century the heart drug digitalis was introduced, scurvy was controlled, surgery was transformed into an experimental science, and reforms were instituted in mental institutions. Edward Jenner introduced vaccination to prevent smallpox, laying the groundwork for the science of immunisation.

● The nineteenth century saw the beginnings of modern medicine when Pasteur, Koch, Ehrlich and Semmelweis proved the relationships between germs and disease. Other developments included: the use of disinfection and the consequent improvement in medical, particularly obstetric, care; inoculation; the introduction of anaesthetics in surgery; and better public health and sanitary measures.

● In the twentieth century Gerhard Domagk discovered the first antibiotic, sulphanilamide, and advancements were made in the use of penicillin. Further progress included: the rise of chemotherapy, especially the use of new antibiotics; greater understanding of the mechanisms of the immune system and the use of vaccination; utilisation of knowledge of the endocrine system to treat diseases resulting from hormone imbalance; and increased understanding of nutrition and the role of vitamins in health. In March 1953, Francis Crick and James Watson announced, 'We have discovered the secret of life.' They had unravelled the chemical structure of the fundamental molecule of heredity, deoxyribonucleic acid (DNA), giving science and medicine the basis for molecular genetics and leading to a continuing revolution in modern medicine.

A delectable selection of ancient diseases
Ague: malarial or intermittent fever characterised by stages of chills, fever, and sweating at regularly recurring times. The disease was popularly known as fever and ague, chill fever, the shakes, and by names expressive of the locality in

which it was prevalent, such as swamp fever in Louisiana and Panama fever.

Cancrum otis: a destructive, eroding ulcer of the cheek and lip. In the nineteenth century it was seen in delicate, ill-fed, ill-tended children between the ages of two and five. The disease was the result of poor hygiene and could, in a few days, lead to gangrene of the lips, cheeks, tonsils, palate, tongue, and even half the face; teeth would fall from their sockets. Also called: canker, water canker, noma, gangrenous stomatitis, and gangrenous ulceration of the mouth.

Consumption: a wasting away of the body; formerly applied especially to pulmonary tuberculosis. Also called marasmus.

Diphtheria: an acute infectious disease acquired by contact with an infected person or a carrier of the disease. It was usually confined to the upper respiratory tract (throat) and characterised by the formation of a tough membrane (false membrane) attached firmly to the underlying tissue that would bleed if forcibly removed.

Effluvia/exhalations. In the mid-nineteenth century, they were called vapours and distinguished into the contagious effluvia, such as rubella (measles); and marsh effluvia, such as miasmata.

Hives: a skin eruption of smooth, slightly elevated areas on the skin that are redder or paler than the surrounding skin. Often attended by severe itching. In the mid-nineteenth century, hives was a commonly given cause of death of children aged three years and under. Because true hives does not kill, croup was probably the actual cause of death in those children.

King's evil: a popular name for scrofula, primary tuberculosis of the lymphatic glands, especially those in the neck. The name originated in the time of Edward the

Confessor, with the belief that the disease could be cured by the touch of the King of England.

Typhus: an acute, infectious disease transmitted by lice and fleas. Also called: typhus fever, malignant fever (in the 1850s), jail fever, hospital fever, ship fever, putrid fever, brain fever, bilious fever, spotted fever, petechial fever, camp fever.

THE FUTURE OF MEDICINE

Where we are today is firmly rooted in the bedrock of medicine and where we go in the future has its roots in the needs of today. Much medical research is now directed toward such problems as cancer, heart disease, AIDS, re-emerging infectious diseases such as tuberculosis and dengue fever, and organ transplantation. Research is an organic product of the health problems that emerge throughout the world.

GENETICS

Currently, the largest worldwide study is the Human Genome Project, which formally began in 1990 and is co-ordinated by the US Department of Energy and the National Institutes of Health. It will identify all hereditary traits and body functions controlled by specific areas on the chromosomes. Gene therapy, the replacement of faulty genes, offers possible abatement of hereditary diseases.

Genetic engineering has led to the development of important pharmaceutical products and the use of monoclonal antibodies, offering promising new approaches to cancer treatment. The discovery of growth factors has opened up the possibility of growth and regeneration of nerve tissues.

The project was originally planned to last 15 years, but rapid technological advances have accelerated the expected completion date to 2003. Project goals are to:

● identify all the 30,000 genes in human DNA

- determine the sequences of the 3 billion chemical base pairs that make up human DNA

- store this information in databases

- improve tools for data analysis

- transfer related technologies to the private sector

- address the ethical, legal, and social issues (ELSI) that may arise from the project.

HOT CAREER MOVES

Clinical cytogeneticist
Clinical scientist in histocompatability/immunogenetics
Doctor in clinical genetics
Ophthalmology
Molecular geneticist
Haematology

PAIN MANAGEMENT

Pain is now recognised as a damaging process in its own right, not just an accompaniment to disease or injury. With its triad of suffering, sleeplessness, and sadness, unrelieved pain causes millions of people to miss work, to become depressed, and to neglect their health. The Joint Commission on Accreditation of Health Organisations and other medical groups have created new standards for assessing and managing pain. Armed with this knowledge, health practitioners and patients are joining forces to create therapies and pain management plans that work. Pain management is a comprehensive treatment approach, in which physicians and patients treat the complex experience of pain with traditional therapies and balance them with complementary and alternative therapies when needed. Medicines such as ibuprofen and aspirin, and complementary and alternative therapies, from acupuncture to yoga, help people to treat the underlying causes of pain as well as the pain itself.

With increased funding and heightened interest in studying both the origins of pain and how patients perceive and deal with it, researchers hope to unravel the causes of pain and devise better ways to treat it.

TROPICAL MEDICINE

Much has been achieved in combating such tropical diseases as yellow fever, amoebic dysentery, and filariasis (elephantiasis). Better public health measures and therapeutic agents have assisted in the fight, and the World Health Organisation (WHO) and philanthropic foundations have helped bring about medical advances.

The deployment of American troops in malaria-infested regions spurred the search for more efficient synthetic antimalarial drugs. DDT, introduced in World War II to eradicate the malaria-carrying mosquito, was found to have lingering toxic effects in the environment, and the persistent use of DDT in China for rice pests produced DDT-resistant mosquitoes. Resistance of the malarial parasite to chloroquine and fansidar, the most widely used drugs for the protection of travellers in the tropics, has made both drugs virtually useless in most of Asia, Africa, and South America. A new drug, mefloquine, is effective in some areas but has many serious side effects.

There have also been advances against hookworm, leprosy, and other tropical maladies. The emergence in central Africa of the Ebola virus, which exists in an as yet unknown host and is fatal to 50–90 per cent of those infected, has been especially challenging to medical personnel.

END-OF-LIFE CARE

As our population lives longer than ever, much focus has been turned to dignity and quality in end-of-life care. Most families are unprepared for the intensity of end-of-life care. By getting information on their loved one's diagnosis, prognosis, and treatment options, they can make sure that their loved one is not in pain and his or her emotional, spiritual, and financial needs are met. With the proper education and training, families and healthcare providers can supply compassionate and holistic end-of-life care.

HOT CAREER MOVES

Nurse
Health visitor
Doctor in palliative medicine
Doctor in geriatrics

SPACE MEDICINE

The principal aim of space medicine is to discover how well and for how long humans can withstand the extreme conditions encountered in space, and how well they can readapt to the earth's environment after a space voyage. The medically significant aspects of space travel include weightlessness, strong inertial forces experienced during lift-off and re-entry, radiation exposure, absence of the earth's day-and-night cycle, and existence in a closed ecological environment. Less critical factors are the noise, vibration, and heat produced within the spacecraft. On longer space flights, the psychological effects of isolation and living in close quarters have been a concern, especially among multinational crews with inherent differences in language and culture.

The development of programmable heart pacemakers, implantable drug administration systems, magnetic resonance imaging (MRI), and computerised axial tomography (CAT) all depended to some extent on knowledge gained from the space programme. Studies of how astronauts would walk in the moon's weak gravitational field led to a deeper understanding of human locomotion.

MULTIPLE SCLEROSIS

This neurological disease has no cure, and its course can be unpredictable. MS strikes people in their 20s and early 30s, a time when many people are starting families and careers. MS is an autoimmune disorder that affects the central nervous system (the brain and spinal cord). Autoimmunity occurs when a person's immune system attacks healthy cells. While the cause of and cure for MS remain unsolved, those affected by the disease have reason to be optimistic about the future. Active research continues on frontiers such as: cellular changes caused by MS as it begins and progresses; more sensitive diagnostic techniques and evaluations; medications that may slow or stop the progression of the disease; therapies to promote the repair of damaged myelin; and treatments to help manage symptoms.

HOT CAREER MOVES

Immunology
Nurse
Health visitor
Doctor in palliative medicine

CLINICAL DEPRESSION

Clinical depression is more than just the blues or the temporary 'down' feeling that most people experience occasionally. It's a biological disorder that can be controlled with medical and psychological help. Major depression is the leading cause of disability in the US and around the world, according to a recent study sponsored by the WHO and the World Bank. Yet millions of people who suffer with the condition aren't even aware they have it, according to the National Institute of Mental Health (NIMH). The problem is sometimes ignored because of feelings of shame or misdiagnosed as another condition. With stepped-up public education and new diagnostic information, mental health professionals hope to help more patients get the treatment they need.

Not only are more effective medications being developed, but researchers are also searching for answers to what causes some people and not others to get depression.

The role of genetics and environmental factors will continue to be studied, along with various treatment options that may help millions of sufferers to manage the condition. To give clinicians better ways to diagnose depression, researchers are working to develop new scanning screening methods and other tools. Researchers will also continue to develop more effective treatments. They'll study combination therapies, alternative treatments (including herbs), light therapy, acupuncture, and diet. In addition, more researchers will search for ways to effectively treat the estimated 20 per cent of patients who are resistant to current treatments.

HOT CAREER MOVES

Psychologist
Psychiatrist

FANCY FINDING OUT MORE?

You can find out more about different areas of health by visiting any number of medical museums, including the following:

Alexander Fleming Laboratory, where Fleming discovered penicillin in 1928. An in-situ reconstruction of the laboratory, displays and a video uncover the story of how a chance discovery became a lifesaving drug that revolutionised medicine. St Mary's Hospital, Praed Street, London W2 1NY. Tel: 020 7886 6528.

Army Medical Services Museum. Keogh Barracks, Ash Vale, Aldershot, Hampshire GU12 5RQ. Tel: 01252 340212.

Association of Anaesthetists. Initially comprising the collection of anaesthetic equipment donated by Charles King, an instrument and anaesthetic appliance designer and manufacturer, the association now holds 2000–3000 artefacts as well as archives, a library, technical literature and films, pictures and slides, all relating to the history of anaesthesia. 21 Portland Place, London W1B 1PY. Tel: 020 7631 8806.

British Optical Association. The premier optical collection in the country, comprising historic spectacles and lenses, pince-nez, opera glasses, opticians' equipment, orthoptic devices, models of eye disease, paintings and prints. The library has an outstanding collection of books on optics and the workings of the human eye from the sixteenth century to the present. College of Optometrists, 42 Craven Street, London WC2N 5NG. Tel: 020 7839 6000.

British Red Cross Museum and Archives record and depict the humanitarian work of the British Red Cross, in peace and in war, from 1870 to today. The collection includes nursing and medical equipment, uniforms, textiles from around the world, medals and badges. 9 Grosvenor Crescent, London, SW1X 7EJ. Tel: 020 7201 5153.

Freud Museum, based in the home of Sigmund Freud and his family after they escaped the Nazi annexation of Austria in 1938. The centrepiece of the museum is Freud's library and study, preserved as it was in his lifetime. It contains his working library, his desk and the famous couch. 20 Maresfield Gardens, London NW3 5SX. Tel: 020 7435 2002.

MedHist (http://medhist.ac.uk) offers free access to a searchable catalogue of Internet sites and resources covering the history of medicine.

Old Operating Theatre and Herb Garret. Hidden in the roof of a church, a 300-year-old herb garret houses the only surviving nineteenth-century operating theatre, complete with wooden operating table and observation stands. The oak-beamed garret was also used for storing and curing medicinal herbs. An interactive tour is available on the website. 9a St Thomas's Street, London SE1 9RY. Tel: 020 7955 4791. Website: www.thegarret.org.uk.

Royal London Hospital Museum, founded in 1740, became Britain's largest voluntary hospital. Its story is told in the crypt of the former Hospital Church. Exhibits feature dentistry, surgery, paediatrics, nursing, the NHS, uniforms, helicopter ambulance, X-rays and videos. Whitechapel, London E1 1BB. Tel: 020 7377 7608.

Royal Pharmaceutical Society Museum's collection traces the story of medicinal drugs from the mysterious apothecary's workshop to twenty-first-century research and mass production. Fine seventeenth-century storage jars, all the equipment of the Victorian dispensary and old patent medicines. 1 Lambeth High Street, London SE1 7JN. Tel: 020 7572 2210.

St Bartholomew's Hospital Museum and Archives. One of the oldest hospitals in the world, St Bartholomew's, or Bart's, was founded in 1123. West Smithfield, London EC1A 7BE. Tel: 020 7601 8152.

Science Museum. Medical collections include clinical medicine, biosciences and public health. Exhibition Road, South Kensington, London SW7 2DD. Tel: 020 7870 4771.

Thackray Medical Museum. Beckett Street, Leeds, West Yorkshire LS9 7LN. Tel: 0113 244 4343. Website: www.thackraymuseum.org.

University of Birmingham Collections. C/o University Curator, Main Library, University of Birmingham, Edgbaston, Birmingham B15 2TT. Tel: 0121 414 6750.

University of Edinburgh Anatomy Museum. Department of Anatomy, University Medical School, Teviot Place, Edinburgh EH8 9AG.

University of Leeds Collections. University of Leeds, Leeds LS2 9JT. Tel: 0113 343 6372. Website: www.leeds.ac.uk/collections.

University of St Andrews Anatomy and Pathology Collection. Bute Medical Building, University of St Andrews, St Andrews, Scotland KY16 9TS. Tel: 01334 462 417.

Worshipful Society of Apothecaries of London. Apothecaries' Hall, Black Friars Lane, London EC4V 6EJ. Tel: 020 7236 1189.

So we have some idea of where medicine has come from. We have an inkling of the potential to come. But are you the person to be part of this exciting future of medicine? Let's find out now.

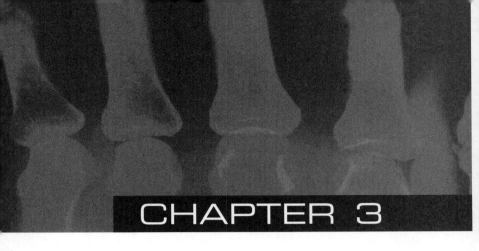

CHAPTER 3

Is Medicine Right for Me?

This chapter looks at some of the key skills and strengths necessary for a career in medicine. At this stage your personal qualities are more important than skills, which can always be learnt at a later stage. See if you've got what it takes.

PERSONAL QUALITIES

Tick any of the following personal qualities that you feel you have:

- awareness of your limitations and knowing when to call for help
- calmness with difficult people
- caring and considerate attitude
- common sense
- confidence
- dedication and enthusiasm
- enquiring mind

- flexibility
- good powers of observation
- high self-motivation
- initiative
- manual dexterity
- maturity and some experience of life
- patience
- physical fitness
- reliability
- self awareness

- self-discipline
- sense of humour
- sense of responsibility
- tact and diplomacy
- tolerance
- trustworthiness.

Personal qualities are crucial if you want a career in medicine. So the more you have ticked, the better it looks.

I see around 50 patients each week, mainly for lower back problems and sports injuries (I work closely with several sports clubs in the area). I see people in my home, their home and once a week at the clinic. I offer both day and evening appointments.

Julia, Osteopath

TRANSFERABLE SKILLS

Tick any of the following transferable skills you have gained through paid or unpaid work (even if you're not dead brill at the skill, it's worth ticking) and enjoy using:

- ability to work unsupervised
- business awareness
- coping with a constantly varying workload
- coping with stress (your own and other people's)
- a critical enquiring approach
- delegation
- drawing information out
- eye for detail
- facing ethical issues
- gathering and using information
- good written and spoken communication
- investigative skills
- IT skills
- leadership and organisation
- listening to and analysing what others are saying
- making sound judgements
- negotiation
- planning
- presentation
- problem-solving
- record-keeping
- self-directed learning
- teaching
- teamwork.

Transferable skills are skills we have an aptitude for, or can learn, and which we can use in any number of occupations, including medicine. The higher the number of ticks, the more optimistic your career in medicine is looking.

After 13 years as a civilian nurse, I joined the service in 1996. At present, I am in charge of the training flight of the aeromedical evaluation squadron within Tactical Medical Wing (TMW) at RAF Lyneham in Wiltshire. My squadron is responsible for flying patients back to the UK from overseas units. As the officer in charge of the training flight, I am tasked with ensuring that all nurses and medics in the RAF successfully complete the flying phase of their aeromed training. I have also worked in The Princess Mary's Hospital (TPMH) at RAF Akrotiri in Cyprus. I was on the adult ward, which meant that there was lots of variety – you could be dealing with anything, from ophthalmics and orthopaedics to surgery and trauma. You just don't get that level of variety in civilian nursing.

Alison, Nursing Officer with the RAF

CHAPTER 4

Roles and Routes into Medicine

This chapter gives an overview of a broad range of occupations in medicine and tells you what education or qualifications you need to get into your dream career.

As you will see, the range is huge. And, although the NHS may be the largest employer of those in medicine, there are many other environments in which you can work. For example, working in dentistry can take you into a hospital environment, the armed forces or the community. You can be a doctor based in a hospital (private or NHS), in the armed forces, a GP or in private practice. Podiatrists (feet specialists) are to be found in beauty salons, on cruise liners, working for places such as Boots, within the NHS or with their own clinic on the high street. A dietician could work in a hospital or be a consultant to a weight management organisation. A psychologist might work for the NHS, for the private sector or in their own practice specialising in, for example, child psychology.

ANAESTHETIST

Anaesthetists make decisions on the best care for a patient to receive not only during an operation but also in the time before and afterwards. Sub-specialisations include cardiac, thoracic, neuro, plastics, paediatrics, obstetrics, trauma and emergency surgery, intensive care medicine and pain management. Anaesthesia is the major specialisation in intensive care medicine (ICM) in Europe; 85 per cent of intensivists in the UK have anaesthesia as their primary specialism. The Royal College of Anaesthetists (RCA) includes training in ICM as part of its syllabus, and a significant proportion of the examinations for the Diploma of Fellowship of the Royal College of Anaesthetists concerns ICM. Exposure to ICM should begin as a senior house officer (SHO), ideally with dedicated blocks of ICM. The primary examination is taken as an SHO and is relevant to practice of ICM.

As a specialist registrar (SpR), sub-specialism blocks including ICM are undertaken. Advanced training in ICM is possible during the elective and research years. However, experience in acute medicine should probably be gained before starting an SpR scheme.

The following schools serve a number of hospitals within their region. Contact each to find out more.

● Coventry School of Anaesthesia, Department of Anaesthesia, Walsgrave Hospitals NHS Trust, Clifford Bridge Road, Walsgrave, Coventry CV2 2DX. Tel: 01203 602020. Website: www.msa.org.uk/CSA.htm.

● Mersey School of Anaesthesia and Perioperative Medicine. Mrs Val Kerwin, Secretary MSAPM, Postgraduate Medical Centre, Thomas Drive, Liverpool L14 3LB. Tel: 0151 282 6609. Email: msa@rlbuh-tr.nwest.nhs.uk. Website: www.msoa.org.uk.

● Northern Schools of Anaesthesia (NSA). There are two schools, which are combined to make up the Northern Schools, based in two main hospitals: Royal Victoria Infirmary in Newcastle; and James Cook University Hospital in Middlesbrough. Contacts: Newcastle School, Northern Schools of Anaesthesia, Anaesthetic Training Department, Royal Victoria Infirmary, Queen Victoria Road, Newcastle upon Tyne, NE1 4LP, UK. Tel: 0191 282 5081. Email: David.Greaves@ncl.ac.uk. Cleveland School, Northern Schools of Anaesthesia, Department of Anaesthesia, James Cook University Hospital, South Tees Hospitals NHS Trust, Marton Road, Middlesbrough, TS4 3BW. Tel: 01642 854601.

Email: ChrisDodds@ea-cdodds.freeserve.co.uk. Website: www.ncl.ac.uk/nsa/index.html.

- South Eastern School of Anaesthesia (SESA) supervises postgraduate specialist training for anaesthesia in South East London, Kent and East Sussex. Anaesthetic Department, Second Floor, New Guy's House, Guy's Hospital, St Thomas's Street, London SE1 9RT. Tel: 01273 771215 or 020 7955 4418. Email: admin@sesa.org.uk. Website: www.sesa.org.uk.

- South West School of Anaesthesia, covering Plymouth, Exeter, Truro, Taunton, Torbay. Website: www.sasak.eurobell.co.uk.

- Welsh School of Anaesthesia, Department of Anaesthetics and Intensive Care Medicine, University of Wales College of Medicine, Heath Park, Cardiff CF14 4XN. Tel: 029 2074 3110. Website: www.uwcm.ac.uk/study/medicine/anaesthetics.

- Wessex School of Anaesthesia co-ordinates the training of anaesthetists in the Wessex half of the South and West Region. Geographically, it covers Portsmouth, Southampton, Poole and Bournemouth, Dorchester and Weymouth, Salisbury, Winchester, Swindon, Basingstoke and the Isle of Wight. Trainees in Bath are allied with the Bristol School. There are no trainees in the Isle of Wight but there is an additional specialist registrar attached to Jersey. Wessex Courses Centre, Postgraduate Dean's Department, South Academic Block, Southampton General Hospital, Tremona Road, Southampton SO16 6YD. Tel: 023 8079 6844. Website: www.anaesthesia-wessex.co.uk.

- Yorkshire East Coast School of Anaesthesia is one of four schools in the Yorkshire Deanery and is based at the departments of anaesthesia in Hull, Grimsby and Scunthorpe. Email: ASaleh@yecsa.org. Website: www.yecsa.org.

Further information: Royal College of Anaesthetists, 48–49 Russell Square, London WC1B 4JP. Tel: 020 7908 7300. Email: info@rcoa.ac.uk. Website: www.rcoa.ac.uk.

ANATOMICAL PATHOLOGY TECHNICIAN

An anatomical pathology technician has a range of responsibilities: record-keeping, maintaining the mortuary and post-mortem room, and ensuring equipment and instruments are clean, sterile and ready to use. He or she helps the pathologist examine the body and take samples for analysis, and after each post mortem prepare the body for storage or collection by undertakers. Anatomical pathology technicians liaise with a range of people, including medical staff, police, and most importantly, relations of those who have died.

There are no minimum entry qualifications for trainee anatomical pathology technicians, although hospitals will often look for some evidence of aptitude in science. Most trainees start straight from school, but older candidates are welcome.

Further information: Royal Institute of Public Health and Hygiene, 28 Portland Place, London W1N 4DE.

ARMY MEDICAL CAREERS

BIOMEDICAL ASSISTANT

The army uses laboratories for a variety of reasons, but one of the main functions is for pathology, where biomedical scientists help medical officers to diagnose diseases by testing substances such as blood samples. Biomedical scientists are based largely in army hospitals in the UK, although there are opportunities to go on operational tours with units around the world.

You need five GCSEs and two A levels, one of which must be in a science subject. Civilians already working as laboratory technicians are also welcome to apply. You can get a BSc (Hons) in biomedical sciences. Age limits: 16–29.

CLINICAL PHYSIOLOGIST

Working in UK hospitals, clinical psychologists do tests that provide doctors with the information they need to make a diagnosis and prescribe treatment or prevent diseases from taking hold in the first place.

You need five GCSEs, grades A–C, including English, maths, physics, chemistry and biology. You can get a BSc (Hons) in MPPM (Medical Physics and Physiological Measurement) and state registration in cardiography and neurophysiology. Age limits: 16–29.

COMBAT MEDICAL TECHNICIAN
The combat medical technician gives emergency treatment, evacuates casualties from the front line and deals with the routine medical needs of soldiers both in conflict and in times of peace. They are employed within medical regiments, medical centres and tri-service hospitals in a support role working under the guidance of medical officers.

Formal academic qualifications may not be necessary. You will receive basic military training, on completion of which you will move to the defence medical services training centre for specialist training. Once you've qualified, you will be posted to one of five medical regiments in the UK or Germany. Age limits: 16–26.

DENTAL HYGIENIST
As a dental hygienist you will be engaged in promoting dental health education with individuals and groups; scaling and polishing teeth; applying medicaments to the surface of the teeth and gums and producing radiographs. You may also administer local infiltration analgesia. Dental hygienists work as part of a dental team, normally in static dental centres. Postings are available in the UK, Germany and Cyprus. On completion of training you will be promoted to lance corporal. After 12 months' service from enlistment, and having passed a corporal's military promotion course and been recommended, you will be promoted to corporal. From then on, promotion is on merit to warrant officer, with the possibility of appointment to commissioned rank. Opportunities exist later in your career to be appointed as a dental hygienist instructor.

You will need a General Dental Council's Diploma in Dental Hygiene. Initial training will teach you military skills. The second part of your training takes place at the Defence Medical Service Training Centre and Defence Dental Agency Training Establishment. This phase covers aspects of dental training, general medical care, including instructions on the completion of military documentation and other administrative procedures. Age limits: 16–30.

DENTAL SUPPORT SPECIALIST (DENTAL NURSE)

You will be trained to assist the dental surgeon at the chair side and to perform administrative duties within the dental centre. Responsibilities include: maintenance of surgery equipment and the preparation, sterilisation and care of instruments; preparation of materials used in the practice of dentistry; processing dental radiographs; and reception duties. You will be employed in military dental centres or hospitals.

A good level of secondary education is required and possession of a dental nurse qualification would be an advantage. Applicants wishing to be considered for training as dental hygienist at a later date will require five GCSEs (grades A–C), or equivalent; relevant subjects include physics, chemistry, biology, maths, English and integrated science. Initial training will teach you military skills. The second part of your training takes place at the Defence Medical Service Training Centre and Defence Dental Agency Training Establishment. This phase covers aspects of dental training, general medical care and instruction on the completion of military documentation and other administrative procedures. Age limits: 16–30.

DENTAL TECHNICIAN

Dental technicians are employed in the construction of all types of dental appliances – acrylic and chrome cobalt dentures, crowns and bridges, implants, orthodontic appliances, splints for fractured jaws, and more complicated appliances for the treatment of facial injuries. They are employed in the main dental laboratory in Aldershot, medical units such as hospitals in the UK, or army dental centres in Germany and Cyprus.

A BTEC in Dental Technology Material Science is required for entry. Initial training will teach you military skills. The second part of your training will take place at the Defence Medical Service Training Centre, and Defence Training Agency Establishment. This training will cover aspects of dental training, general medical care, and instruction on the completion of military documentation and other administrative procedures. Age limits: 16–30.

ENVIRONMENTAL HEALTH TECHNICIAN

The role of the environmental health technician is to work under the supervision of the environmental health officer supervising and advising on all matters of environmental health. This includes accommodation, field sanitation, water supplies, food hygiene, pest control, prevention and control of pollution, health education, health and safety at work.

You need GCSE grades A–C, or equivalent, in four subjects: English language, maths and two sciences. On completion of basic military training you will move to the Defence Medical Services Training Centre for specialist training, which lasts some five months. Age limits: 16–26.

HEALTH CARE ASSISTANT

Health care assistants in the Queen Alexandra's Royal Army Nursing Corps (QAs) care for soldiers, their families and civilians. You will be trained to perform certain tasks such as bathing and dressing patients; feeding patients; taking patients' temperatures, pulse and blood pressure; assisting patients to mobilise; assisting patients to use toilet facilities and escorting patients around the hospital.

Evidence of a sound secondary education is required for entry. Age limits: 17–32.

OPERATING DEPARTMENT PRACTITIONER

The role of the operating department practitioner is to maintain ideal operating conditions and preventing operating theatre accidents. You will assist both the surgeon and the anaesthetist.

Academic qualifications include two subjects at A level, supported by three GCSE passes (grades A–C). On completion of basic training you will move to the Royal Defence Medical College Gosport for specialist training, which lasts some six months. Age limits: 16–26.

PHARMACY TECHNICIAN

The pharmacy technician is responsible for drugs and medical materials in hospitals and medical centres. You will be responsible for dispensing medical preparations for individual patients and supply stocks for wards from a hospital medical store or medical depot.

Five GCSEs at grades A–C or equivalent, in English, maths, biology and one or more other sciences are required. On completion of your basic training you will go to the Royal Defence Medical College Gosport for specialist training, which lasts six months. Age limits: 16–26.

RADIOGRAPHER

Radiographers use sophisticated imaging equipment to help doctors make diagnoses. They work either in modern, well-serviced departments or in minimal conditions, with more basic equipment, in the field.

You need five GCSEs at grade C or higher, including English, maths and physics, as well as 16 points at A level, including one science subject. Applicants with a diploma from the College of Radiographers or a BSc (Hons) in diagnostic radiography can also apply. What you can get is state registration as a radiographer. Age limits: 16–29.

REGISTERED NURSE (ADULT, MENTAL HEALTH)

Nurses in the QAs care for soldiers, their families and civilians. The main responsibilities of the staff nurse are to nurse all the patients in their care, ensuring all nursing is carried out to a high standard, and to teach and supervise health care assistants. After one year in the QAs there are opportunities to take post - registration courses in specialised fields. Once recruit training is completed you will be posted to a hospital in the UK, but you may find yourself anywhere in the world. As a qualified nurse you will be eligible for promotion.

You must be a qualified registered general nurse (adult). Age limits: 21–38.

STUDENT NURSE (ADULT OR MENTAL HEALTH)

This is a three-year training course for qualification as a registered nurse (adult) with a Diploma in Higher Education. You will need five

GCSEs at grade C or above, including English language, mathematics or a science-based subject. You will receive basic military training. On successful completion of this training, you go to the University of Portsmouth to train as a nurse. After an 18-month common foundation programme, army students move on to the adult branch training programme. Age limits: 17–38.

Further information: Army website: www.army.mod.uk/careers.

CLINICAL BIOCHEMIST

Clinical biochemists develop and manage hospital and community analytical services, and provide data interpretation and advice needed for the diagnosis of disease, and for planning and monitoring its treatment. In most departments, the clinical biochemist also devises and carries out basic or applied research, often working with medical colleagues. Clinical biochemists should become expert in a particular specialist area, such as endocrinology or toxicology, paediatrics, immunology and molecular biochemistry. In departments based in university teaching hospitals, clinical biochemists employed by the NHS are likely to have close links with their university colleagues, and possibly honorary status within the university department, involving them in teaching and academic research.

A good honours degree in biochemistry or chemistry is needed to enter the NHS as a trainee clinical biochemist. Members and graduate members of the Royal Society of Chemistry and members of the Institute of Biologists are also eligible. An MSc in clinical biochemistry or a related subject is a valuable asset and some entrants also have a PhD.

Further information: Recruitment Centre for Clinical Scientists, Northgate, Wrest House, Wrest Park, Silsoe, Bedfordshire MK45 4HG. Tel: 01525 863605. Email: clinicalscientist@northgate-is.com.

CLINICAL CYTOGENETICIST

Clinical cytogeneticists study chromosomes obtained from samples of patients' blood, tissue, bone marrow or other body tissue or fluid. Their expert knowledge of chromosome irregularities is invaluable to clinicians for the diagnosis of genetic disease. The laboratory genetics service is mainly organised on a regional basis, and the scientists work in hospital laboratories.

Graduates in genetics or a variety of life sciences are eligible for entry into the Grade A training programme. Some candidates obtain a higher degree before entry.

Further information: Recruitment Centre for Clinical Scientists (contact details above).

CLINICAL EMBRYOLOGIST

The laboratory work carried out by clinical embryologists is a fundamental part of any IVF or related programme of assisted reproduction. They critically examine individual cases using a variety of processes and research possible solutions. Such tasks may include egg collection, checking fertilisation and embryo implanting.

A good degree in a biological science is the usual entry qualification.

Further information: Recruitment Centre for Clinical Scientists (contact details above).

CLINICAL ENGINEER

Clinical engineers use physical and materials sciences and manufacturing skills to help diagnose and treat disease, and rehabilitate patients with disabilities. Some clinical engineers design and develop instruments for patient monitoring, diagnosis, treatment or research. Joint replacements, active implants and tools for minimally invasive (keyhole) or precision (robotic) surgery are built and tested in clinical engineering laboratories. Some clinical engineers work in large departments that also cover a range of medical physics activities. Others may form the scientific nucleus of a rehabilitation unit that includes doctors, nurses and therapists.

The minimum qualification is normally an honours degree in physical or engineering science. A higher degree or industrial experience may be valuable.

Further information: Recruitment Centre for Clinical Scientists (contact details above).

CLINICAL IMMUNOLOGIST

Scientists in clinical immunology use complex equipment and sophisticated molecular techniques. They work with clinicians, both in general practice and in hospital-based specialisms, to develop new tests and treatments involving manipulation of the immune system. Clinical immunology is a relatively new specialism within the NHS. There are as yet only a few designated clinical immunology laboratories in each NHS region.

A good honours degree in a relevant biological science, or a combined sciences degree with a major element of biochemistry and/or immunology.

Further information: Recruitment Centre for Clinical Scientists (contact details above).

CLINICAL MICROBIOLOGIST

Clinical microbiologists help to diagnose infections in individuals, and to prevent and control infections in the community and within hospitals. They are employed in diagnostic laboratories and pathology departments in larger hospitals and university medical schools. The Public Health Laboratory Service is the major employer of clinical scientists in microbiology, many of whom work in reference laboratories, and some as epidemiologists. Clinical microbiologists are often responsible for more complex and specialised techniques and play an important part in the development of new or better diagnostic tests, and in fundamental or applied research programmes in bacteriology, virology, mycology and parasitology, often in collaboration with clinical or industrial colleagues.

The minimum qualification is an honours degree in microbiology or another relevant biological discipline.

Further information: Recruitment Centre for Clinical Scientists (contact details above).

CLINICAL ONCOLOGIST

Clinical oncology embraces the non-surgical aspect of oncology. It involves both radiotherapy and cytotoxic chemotherapy. Radiotherapy is the administration of ionising radiation, predominantly by external beam (teletherapy), but it may also involve the more technical operative implantation of interstitial sources, which are often after-loaded with radioactive material, e.g. iridium. Consultants are increasingly site-specialised and are based in a cancer centre, often visiting peripheral cancer units. This specialism gives the opportunity of developing clinical and scientific skills with great potential for academic and clinical research. There are also increasing opportunities to take part in national and international research trials.

In the UK doctors enter training in clinical oncology after one post-registration year and at least two years in general medicine. People are admitted to the training programme on completion of a higher degree in a training centre accredited by the Royal College of Radiologists.

Further information: the Royal College of Radiologists sets the standards and curriculum for specialist training in clinical oncology. An information pack for those considering UK specialist training in clinical oncology is available from Beverley Maxey, Training Administrator. Tel: 020 7636 4432 ext. 123. Email: beverley_maxey@rcr.ac.uk. When requesting the information pack, please provide a full postal address and the name of the medical school from which you graduated.

CLINICAL PHYSIOLOGIST

You will work closely with patients to provide a range of specialist services and will be responsible for the measurement and monitoring of physiological parameters to provide information to doctors and consultants on the extent of disease or disability. The role involves measuring, evaluating and recording the capacity of various parts of the body to function normally. Medical staff then use these results to assess patients' health and to help to manage disease and disability. The job also involves testing and adjusting equipment and teaching patients how to use it. The job would also require you to work in many different departments of the hospital and in various community clinics.

NHS Pay (April 2002)

Grade A (main training grade)	£14,650–£19,280
Grade B (main professional grade)	£20,050–£37,560
Grade C (top grade)	£36,120–£60,140

AUDIOLOGICAL SCIENTIST

Audiology involves investigating disorders of hearing and balance, particularly in young children, the elderly and those exposed to industrial noise. Audiological scientists ensure that reliable and valid test techniques are used, develop and assess new tests, and conduct research on diagnostic and rehabilitative corrective services for the hearing-impaired. Most audiological scientists work in an audiological department comprising medical, scientific, technical, therapeutic and educational personnel. Some work in medical physics departments.

An honours degree in a behavioural or physical science is required, or other qualification acceptable for entry into an MSc course in audiology.

Further information: Recruitment Centre for Clinical Scientists (contact details on p. 30).

AUDIOLOGIST

Audiological technicians work in hospitals, using and maintaining the equipment used to diagnose and treat patients. Many work closely with patients, but some spend most of their time working on the equipment. They will work in the hospital audiology department and form part of a team with the doctors, nurses and others responsible for the care of the patient.

Although there are no minimum entry qualifications for some posts within NHS trusts, this profession is moving towards graduate entry. The usual entry requirement to the BSc will be three A levels. However, universities will consider each application individually and credit can be given for relevant experience and non-traditional qualifications. For degree courses, apply through Universities and Colleges Admission Service (UCAS).

Further information: Recruitment Centre for Clinical Scientists (contact details on p. 30), or you can visit the Clinical Scientists website, www.nhsclinicalscientists.info, where you will also be able to apply online.

CARDIAC PHYSIOLOGIST/CARDIAC CLINICAL SCIENTIFIC OFFICER

These professionals perform a range of investigations and treatments on patients with cardiac disease. They record heart rhythm, measure electrical activity in the heart, compare blood circulation in various parts of the body, analyse blood gases, and record blood pressure. Other important elements of the job include monitoring a patient's heart condition during surgery or in intensive care.

Although there are at present no minimum entry qualifications, employing authorities will usually expect qualifications acceptable for college or university. There will in the future be a formal requirement for entrants to the profession to be graduates in an appropriate degree, e.g. clinical physiology (cardiology).

Further information: Society for Cardiological Science and Technology, 9 Fitzroy Square, London W1P 5AH. Website: www.scst.org.uk.

CARDIOGRAPHER

Cardiographers support the work of cardiology physiologists and cardiac clinical scientific officers by performing routine recordings of the electrical activity of the heart at rest (electrocardiograms), which constitute a significant proportion of the workload in a cardiac department. They also assist their technical colleagues in the attachment of recorders, which record the electrocardiogram for 24 hours, and prepare patients for ECG exercise testing.

Cardiographers do not usually require formal entry qualifications, but are encouraged to become enrolled members of the Society

for Cardiological Science and Technology (SCST) and undertake
the Certificate in Electrocardiography examination.

Further information: Society for Cardiological Science and
Technology (contact details above).

GASTROENTEROLOGY TECHNICIAN

Gastroenterology technicians measure pressure, pressure changes
and acidity along the entire length of the alimentary canal. The
readings are then interpreted. This can be in a variety of
circumstances, for example after different kinds of meals or drugs.

Although there are no minimum entry qualifications, employing
authorities will usually expect qualifications acceptable for college
or university – four GCSEs (grade C or above), a science A Level or
a BTEC National Award in electronics – or a degree in engineering.

Further information: contact the HR/personnel department of your
local hospital trust.

HEARING THERAPIST

A hearing therapist's role is to provide a comprehensive
rehabilitation service for adults with hearing difficulties and/or
associated disorders. Aural rehabilitation services can include
explaining hearing difficulties, supporting people who have a
sudden loss of hearing, auditory training, lip
reading/communication tactics, relaxation, balance rehabilitation,
support to people undergoing cochlear implants, working with
people with learning disabilities or a dual sensory impairment and
giving information about environmental equipment.

Minimum entry requirements: two A levels in science subjects,
and applications are welcome from people with higher
qualifications or a science degree.

Further information: contact the HR/personnel department of your
local hospital trust.

NEUROPHYSIOLOGY TECHNICIAN

Neurophysiology technicians attach electrodes from an
electroencephalograph (EEG) and other machines to patients and

read the results from a screen or printout. They are responsible for setting up and operating electronic equipment that records electrical activity of the brain and the nervous system. They help to diagnose diseases such as epilepsy, strokes, dementia, muscular dystrophy and multiple sclerosis.

There are no minimum entry qualifications, but employing authorities will usually expect qualifications acceptable for college or university – four GCSEs (grade C or above), a science A Level or a BTEC National Award in electronics – or a degree in engineering.

Further information: contact the HR/personnel department of your local hospital trust.

OPERATING DEPARTMENT PRACTITIONER (ODP)

The principal role is to ensure that the right surgical instruments and dressings are available, and to pass them to the surgeon as they are needed. The ODP checks the instrument trays before the operation and keeps track of all swabs and dressings used as the operation progresses. As the operation ends, the ODP checks that no dressings or instruments have been left in the patient, and signs a register to confirm this. They might also help prepare the patient, ensure the right medical records are available, and bring in any additional equipment the theatre team might need. ODPs prepare equipment and instruments for local or general anaesthetics to be given; they also take responsibility for the drugs that are used. Whilst most ODPs are based in operating theatres, anaesthetic areas and recovery rooms, some work with accident and emergency departments, intensive care units and cardiac arrest teams, where their skills – especially in assisting anaesthetics – are valuable. Experience in other types of hospital work – for example as a healthcare assistant or nursing auxiliary – will help prepare you for the ODP role.

ODP training leads to a Diploma in Higher Education undertaken at a higher education institution, so the minimum entry requirements for training will vary and be set by the individual institution. Applicants are routinely subject to health and criminal record screening (to protect both patients and applicants) as part of the application process.

Further information: contact the HR/personnel department of your local hospital trust.

PERFUSIONIST

As a clinical perfusionist, you would be a key member of the cardiac surgical team, working with surgeons, the anaesthetist, theatre nurses and other support staff. You will be controlling the activity of machines that pump blood around the patient's body and replace carbon dioxide with oxygen in the patient's bloodstream. Because of their unique skills, clinical perfusionists are also involved in a range of activities that involve blood processing techniques, monitoring vital parameters, and interpreting blood gas and chemistry. Some are engaged in research.

Trained clinical perfusionists will have high-level scientific ability. Minimum entry requirements are two A levels in science subjects, and applications are welcome from people with higher qualifications or a science degree.

Further information: contact the HR/personnel department of your local hospital trust or get in touch with the Chief Perfusionist, Society of Perfusionists of Great Britain and Ireland. Email: societyofperfusionists@sopgbi.org. Vacancies for trainee perfusionists may be advertised in the *New Scientist* or *Perfusionist*.

RESPIRATORY PHYSIOLOGY TECHNICIAN

Respiratory physiology technicians perform investigations to help diagnose respiratory disorders such as asthma and emphysema. A variety of highly specialised equipment is used to determine the volume of the lungs and how well they function. Additional tests include sensitivity to allergens and exercise. Many departments also perform more complex tests whereby patients are monitored during sleep to discover sleep-related breathing disorders.

Although there are no minimum entry qualifications, employing authorities will usually expect qualifications acceptable for college or university – four GCSEs (grade C or above), a science A Level or a BTEC National Award in electronics – or a degree in engineering.

Further information: contact the HR/personnel department of your local hospital trust.

CLINICAL RADIOLOGIST

Diagnostic imaging is probably one of the most rapidly expanding specialisations of recent years. Radiology acts as a significant aid in the diagnosis, management and follow-up of many patients from almost all medical specialisms. There are the additional benefits of working within single radiological departments and the association with many levels of staff necessary in making that department function coherently. The potential of ultrasound, CT and more particularly MR, is yet to be developed and therefore these challenges remain. As well as being responsible for the management of the imaging departments, radiologists are intimately involved in clinical teams. Differing levels of management involvement can be entered into, and private practice opportunities are usually good.

In the UK, doctors can only enter training in clinical radiology when they have obtained a minimum of two years' experience in an acceptable clinical specialisation, usually one of the general medical or general surgical disciplines. The trainee radiologist will be appointed to a specialist registrar post in a training centre accredited for training by the Royal College of Radiologists.

Further information: Royal College of Radiologists (contact details on p. 33).

CLINICAL SCIENTIST IN HISTOCOMPATABILITY AND IMMUNOGENETICS

When a kidney, heart, liver or other organ is to be transplanted from a donor into a patient, the immunogenetic characteristics of donor and recipient have to be determined and matched. Clinical scientists in the histocompatibility or 'tissue typing' laboratory are responsible not only for the practical laboratory science, but also for the logistics of keeping registers of the immunogenetic status of potential recipients. They have the main responsibility for advising clinicians on the most suitably tissue-matched patient in

each case. Scientists in this field may be located in an
independent hospital department, a blood transfusion centre or
genetics department, or even in a department of transplant
surgery.
Requirements include a minimum second class degree in the
biomedical sciences (e.g. biochemistry, genetics or immunology).
Further information: Recruitment Centre for Clinical Scientists
(contact details on p. 30).

CLINICAL SCIENTIST IN IMMUNOLOGY

Immunology is a rapidly developing clinical science, which
contributes to the diagnosis and management of patients with
allergy, primary and secondary immunodeficiency and
autoimmune diseases, and also to the success of organ
transplantation. The immunologist can be directly responsible for
the clinical diagnosis and treatment of patients with
immunological conditions. The types of patient under his/her care
depend on local needs and the interests of the individual
consultant, but would typically include immunodeficiency and
allergy. Combined clinics, run in conjunction with consultants
from other specialisms, extend the range of patients seen.
Clinical laboratory work forms an important part of the
immunologist's remit.

For state registration you must possess a first or second class
honours degree in a relevant science subject, after which you
could take one of two routes:

1   Three-year training scheme for Grade A clinical scientists in
    immunology. One year of experience and further training
    while practising as a supervised pre-registrant in an approved
    clinical immunology laboratory.

2   Three years' relevant postgraduate experience in a clinical
    science. Three years of experience and further training while
    practising as a supervised pre-registrant in an approved
    clinical immunology laboratory.

Further information: Recruitment Centre for Clinical Scientists
(contact details on p. 30); Clinical Scientists' website (see p. 30).

Clinical scientists' pay (April 2002)

Grade A (training grade)	£15,790–£19,900
Grade B (main professional grade)	£20,700–£38,900
Grade C (top grade)	£37,400–£62,300

CYTOSCREENER

Cytoscreeners are trained to recognise normal cells and to pass on any smears that seem abnormal to biomedical scientists. If abnormalities are confirmed, a specialised doctor will then be called in. Cytoscreeners are always supervised by state-registered medical laboratory scientific officers (MLSOs), and ultimately by the consultant cytopathologist.

There are no formal educational or age requirements to train as a cytoscreener. You must have, or gain through your practical training, the minimum entry requirements (four GCSEs, or equivalent experience) to take the NHS Cervical Screening Programme (NHSCSP) Certificate in Cervical Cytology.

Further information:

● British Society of Clinical Cytology. Website: www.bscc@cansearch.org.uk.

● Institute of Biomedical Science, 12 Coldbath Square, London EC1R 5HL. Tel: 020 7713 0214. Website: ww.ibms.org.

DENTIST

GENERAL DENTAL SERVICE (GDS)/PERSONAL DENTAL SERVICE (PDS)

In order to work in NHS general practice or as an associate in their own dental practice, a dentist must enter their name on the dental list of the Primary Care Trust for the area in which they will be working. For those qualifying at a UK dental school, this requires completion of one year's vocational training (VT). A vocational dental practitioner works in an approved training practice under supervision and also receives additional training of specific relevance to general or community dental practice. On completion of the VT, the dentist is issued with a VT number by the Dental

Vocational Training Authority (DVTA), which enables them to be entered on the NHS dental list. Following vocational training, dentists usually enter an established general practice as an associate or as an assistant. An associate is a self-employed dentist, responsible for the treatment that they provide but working in a practice owned by someone else. In some areas, a number of practices prefer to employ assistant dentists. An assistantship provides an opportunity to work as a full member of the practice team but without the uncertainties of a role as an associate.

A dentist may often become a practice owner or partner. Like GPs, they have the opportunity to form long-term relationships with their patients and provide them with continuing care. As well as an ability to get on well with people and for clinical dentistry, it is essential to have an aptitude for business, since the dentist is a manager and team leader running a small business.

Pay scales (April 2002): vocational dental practitioners are paid a salary of £24,970 during their vocational training year; typical earnings for a full-time, self-employed general dental practitioner (GDP) are around £75,000 to £80,000 a year.

HOSPITAL DENTISTRY

Unlike general dental practitioners, hospital dentists receive a salary. They generally work as part of a team, have access to specialised diagnostic facilities and work with consultants in other specialisms. However, the hours are not as flexible and time will be spent on call. Within the hospital service there is a defined career structure and training pathway, and advancement requires obtaining recognised postgraduate qualifications.

PAY SCALES (APRIL 2002)

- Senior house officer (SHO) working directly with patients as part of a team. Basic salary: £25,000. Typical earnings: £40,000.

- Specialist registrar (SpR) working in a chosen area of special knowledge and expertise for 4–6 years or longer (could include a period of medical research). Basic salary: £33,000. Typical earnings: £52,000.

- Consultant, leader of a dental team and responsible for the treatment of patients seen by that team. Typical earnings: from £52,600 upwards.

COMMUNITY DENTAL SERVICE (CDS)

As with the hospital service, these posts are salaried. Dentists wishing to work in the CDS must normally undertake a period of vocational training as outlined above for dentists wishing to work in the GDS. In London and the South East, there is a dedicated CDS VT scheme. Having completed vocational training, experience is gained as a Community Clinical Dental Officer (CCDO) with further opportunity to gain postgraduate qualifications by part-time study. An ambitious CCDO may wish to become a Senior Dental Officer (SDO), with a special responsibility (e.g. for health promotion; epidemiology or treating patients with special needs). For information on this particular scheme, contact the Postgraduate Deans Department, 33 Millman Street, London WC1M 3JH. Tel: 020 7692 3232/7692 3100.

PAY SCALES (APRIL 2002)

- Senior house officer (SHO). Basic salary: £25,000. Typical earnings: £40,000.

- Specialist registrar (SpR) working in a chosen area of special knowledge and expertise 4–6 years or longer. Basic salary: £33,020. Typical earnings: £52,000.

Applicants will usually need three science A levels at grades AAA to ABB, including chemistry, or two science A levels including chemistry and maths, as well as supporting GCSEs.

This job allows so much freedom. Most dentists are self-employed so you can choose your hours and where you work. We're 1,000 dentists short in the UK, so I know I'll get a job wherever I go.

Judith, Self-Employed Dentist

For students studying the new post-16 qualifications in England and Wales, it is likely that entry requirements will be similar to the following: at least 21 units completed that may include a combination of A, AS, GNVQ and key skills. Twelve units will need to be full A levels at grades A or B, where one must be chemistry or biology and the second should be from the group: chemistry, biology, physics, mathematics and statistics. If not offered at A level, then chemistry or biology must be offered at AS level, grade B. The remaining 9 units could be offered in science or non-science subjects. It is likely that general studies will not be accepted at either A or AS level. Three units could be key skills at Level 3. A minimum of 360 points must be achieved.

Candidates normally need GCSE/S grade (A–C/1–3) in English, and many dental schools ask for physics, mathematics and biology at this level. Candidates from Scotland need five H grades with typical grades of AAAAB, including chemistry. Some dental schools require passes or grade B in Certificate of Sixth Year Studies. Students studying Advanced Highers are likely to be asked for three Advanced Highers to include chemistry and another science or mathematics, and specified supporting Highers, Standard Grade and Intermediate passes.

The dental school will consider individually mature applicants who have undertaken a kite-marked Access course.

Applicants with a degree will normally need to get an upper-second class degree and must have A level grades close to the institution's standard requirements.

All dentists in the UK initially follow the same education and training. A candidate initially needs to obtain a bachelor's degree (either a BDS or BChD) from a dental school. Further training related to the specialism chosen then follows this.

The following universities have schools of dentistry offering a pre-dental year. These are for candidates with non-science subjects to offer at A level (or equivalent). The pre-dental year is a preliminary course in chemistry, physics and biology, normally lasts 30 weeks and immediately precedes the five-year degree course:

- Bristol Dental School, University of Bristol, Lower Maudlin Street, Bristol BS1 2LY. Tel: 0117 923 0050. Website: www.dent.bris.ac.uk.

- Dundee University Dental School, Park Place, Dundee DD1 4HN. Tel: 01382 660 111. Website: www.dundee.ac.uk/dentalschool.

- King's College School of Medicine and Dentistry, Denmark Hill, London SE5 8RX. Tel: 020 7737 4000. Website: www.kcl.ac.uk/depsta/acadeu.html.

- University of Manchester (The Turner Dental School), Higher Cambridge Street, Manchester M15 6FH. Tel: 0161 275 6666. Website: www.den.man.ac.uk.

- University of Wales Dental School, Heath Park, Cardiff CF4 4XY. Tel: 01222 747747. Website: www.uwcm.ac.uk/study/dentistry/index.htm.

Standard dental courses last five years and include academic education combined with theoretical and practical training. The academic requirements for entrance to dental school vary according to the school and should be checked individually. The following dental schools provide the five-year degree courses in dentistry:

- Birmingham Dental School, University of Birmingham, Edgbaston, Birmingham B15 2TT. Tel: 0121 414 3344. Website: www.bham.ac.uk.

- Bristol Dental School (contact details above).

- Dundee University Dental School (contact details above).

- Glasgow University Dental School, 378 Sauchiehall Street, Glasgow G2 3JZ. Tel: 0141 211 9600. Website: www.gla.ac.uk/Acad/Dental.

- Guy's, King's and St Thomas's Dental Institute, Hodgkin Building, Guy's Campus, St Thomas's Street, London SE1 1UL. Tel: 020 7848 6963. Website: www.kcl.ac.uk/depsta/dentistry.

- Leeds University School of Dentistry, Clarendon Way, Leeds LS2 9LU. Tel: 0113 244 0111. Website: www.leeds.ac.uk/dental/dental.html.

- University of Liverpool School of Dental Surgery, University of Liverpool, PO Box 147, Pembroke Place, Liverpool L3 5PS. Tel: 0151 706 2000. Website: www.liv.ac.uk/~luds.

- University of Manchester (contact details above).

- University of Newcastle upon Tyne, The Dental School, Framlington Place, Newcastle upon Tyne NE2 4BW. Tel: 0191 222 6000. Website: http://medical.faculty.ncl.ac.uk/dentistry/index_html.

- Medical Faculty, Queen's University of Belfast, University Road, Belfast BT7 1NN. Tel: 028 9033 5081. Email: admissions@qub.ac.uk. Website: www.qub.ac.uk.

- Royal London Hospital Medical College Dental School, Turner Street, London E1 2AD. Tel: 020 7377 7000. Website: www.mds.qmw.ac.uk.

- Sheffield School of Clinical Dentistry, University of Sheffield, Charles Clifford Dental Hospital, Wellesley Road, Sheffield S10 2SZ. Tel: 0114 271 7800. Website: www.shef.ac.uk/uni/academic/D-H/dentsch.

- University of Wales Dental School (contact details above).

Department of Health bursaries cover tuition fees and maintenance costs and clinical placement costs or travelling expenses.

Students eligible for funding will receive this in due course from the NHS Student Grants Unit (SGU). Each dental school provides the NHS SGU with details of students to whom funding eligibility applies. The NHS SGU sends bursary application forms directly to these students, and the completed forms must be sent back to the NHS SGU.

For the first four years, support for English domiciled students on undergraduate dental courses will be on the same basis as for other higher education students – through their Local Education Authority (LEA). From year five onwards, tuition fees will be paid by the Department of Health and a means-tested bursary will be made available in addition to the standard maintenance loan from the Student Loans Company.

Graduates taking a standard five-year course will be entitled to receive student loans for their maintenance. If they have previously taken a publicly funded higher education course lasting two years or more, they will not be entitled to receive funding for tuition fees from their local authorities, and universities may charge them the full cost of their tuition. (Fees payable to dental schools by graduate students vary widely and details are available from the schools themselves.) From year five onwards, tuition fees will be paid by the Department of Health and a means-tested bursary will be made available in addition to the standard maintenance loan from the Student Loans Company.

For further general information on student funding, students should consult the booklet *Financial Help for Healthcare Students*. Contact NHS Careers on 0845 606 0655 to order a copy. Individual dental schools will be able to provide students with advice about the process for applying for bursaries as appropriate.

Further information:

● British Dental Association (BDA), 64 Wimpole Street, London W1G 8YS. Tel: 020 7563 4563. Email: enquiries@bda-dentistry.org.uk. Website: www.bda-dentistry.org.uk.

● British Society of Paediatric Dentistry. Website: www.bda-dentistry.org.uk/bspd.

● Dental Vocational Training Authority (DVTA), Masters House, Temple Grove, Compton Place, Eastbourne East Sussex BN20 8AD. Tel: 01323 431 189.

● Faculty of Dental Surgery (also Joint Committee for Specialist Training in Dentistry (JCSTD) and National Advice Centre for

Postgraduate Dental Education (NACPDE)), Royal College of Surgeons of England, 25–43 Lincoln's Inn Fields, London WC2A 3PN. Tel: 020 7869 6810. Website: www.rcseng.ac.uk. Email: fds@rcseng.ac.uk.

● Faculty of Dental Surgery, Royal College of Surgeons of Edinburgh, Nicolson Street, Edinburgh EH8 9DW. Tel: 0131 556 6206. Website: www.rcsed.ac.uk. Email: information@rcsed.ac.uk.

● General Dental Council (GDC), 37 Wimpole Street, London W1G 8DQ. Tel: 020 7887 3800. Website: www.gdc-uk.org.

DIETICIAN

Dieticians inform the general public about nutrition, evaluate treatments, and educate clients, health professionals and community groups. They can work in a variety of areas, for example in hospitals or in the community as clinical dieticians, health educators or as managers. You can specialise in a clinical area, such as oncology or gastroenterology, or work with a particular group, such as elderly people or those with learning difficulties. Teaching or health education are also options, or you could take on a management role, eventually being responsible for controlling a budget and planning and marketing a dietetic service.

NHS Pay (April 2002)

Newly qualified dietitian	£17,115–£19,155
Senior II	£18,375–£23,405
Senior I	£21,825–£26,055
Chief Head Superint III	£21,825–£27,600
Allied Health Professions (AHPs) Consultant	£33,940–£46,675

Five GCSEs including maths and English, or the equivalent, and at least two relevant A levels, or equivalent, are required for entry to the degree course. An alternative is a first degree in a relevant science for entry to a postgraduate diploma course.

Further information: British Dietetic Association, 5th Floor, Charles House, 148/149 Great Charles Street, Queensway, Birmingham B3 3HT. Email: info@bda.uk.com. Website: www.bda.uk.com.

DOCTOR

As a doctor of medicine, you could specialise in a wide range of roles.

GENERAL PRACTITIONER (GP)

GPs usually work for Primary Care Trusts (PCTs). PCTs are groups of primary care providers, which may include several GP surgeries, a clinic and other healthcare professionals such as opticians or pharmacists. The bulk of the work is carried out during consultations in the surgery and during home visits. There are opportunities to become involved in hospital work, e.g. as a clinical assistant, in the education of those training to be general practitioners or in local issues, e.g. new primary care groups. Individual general practitioners can reach a relatively high income early in their career and it is one of the specialisms most suited for part-time and flexible working. Most GPs are independent contractors to the NHS. This independence means that they are usually responsible for providing adequate premises from which to practise, and for employing their own staff.

ACCIDENT AND EMERGENCY (A&E)

A&E medicine is an expanding specialism. A&E doctors are generalists who specialise in resuscitation. A number also develop their own sub-specialism interests. There are close working links between general practitioners, the local ambulance service, in-patient hospital specialisms and the A&E department.

ALLERGY

Allergy is a clinical specialty with scientific roots in immunology. Because it overlaps with several organ-based specialities, particularly respiratory medicine, dermatology and ENT, it requires knowledge of aspects of these specialities. It shares with immunology many of the same laboratory techniques, but those who practise clinically in the specialism are unlikely to be called upon to direct service laboratory departments. They may, however, run research laboratories.

AUDIOLOGICAL MEDICINE

This includes all aspects of the investigation, diagnosis, and management of hearing-impaired and balance-disordered children and adults, as well as children with communication disorders.

CARDIOLOGY

Cardiology is a clinically based specialism, which encompasses the diagnosis, assessment and management of patients with cardiovascular disease. Most consultants divide their time between in-patient and out-patient clinical duties, including coronary care and investigative/interventional procedures. Sub-specialisms include non-invasive cardiology, interventional cardiology and electrophysiology.

CLINICAL GENETICS

Clinical genetics is concerned with the diagnosis of disorders and birth defects caused by genetic mechanisms and with risk estimation and genetic counselling of family members. Clinical geneticists generally work in multi-disciplinary regional genetics centres, along with scientists, genetic associates and academic colleagues. Clinical work is mostly out-patient based, but ward referrals are also seen.

CLINICAL PHARMACOLOGY AND THERAPEUTICS

Most pharmacologists work in teaching hospitals and a substantial part of their work involves teaching. They are also commonly involved in research on the effects of drugs on patients and often run clinics in areas of medicine where therapeutics is important, such as hypertension, cardiovascular medicine and epilepsy. Because their expertise is widely sought after, clinical pharmacologists often find themselves members of drug and therapeutics committees, advisers to health authorities or sitting on regional or national committees that consider prescribing.

DERMATOLOGY

Dermatology is a rapidly developing medical specialism. The variety of sub-specialisms in dermatology is increasing and the amount of work is likely to remain high. Dermatology is also an essential part of general practice and a high proportion of GP consultations are for skin disease. There are opportunities to develop a particular interest in such areas as skin surgery, laser surgery and occupational dermatology.

ENDOCRINOLOGY AND DIABETES MELLITUS

Diabetes and endocrinology is concerned with hormone under- and over-production. It is mainly an out-patient specialty. There is opportunity to develop the care of diabetes in the community with GPs. There is also an increasing involvement in epidemiological research and audit. Many opportunities exist for laboratory-based molecular and cellular research and there are excellent opportunities in academic medicine, while the traditional discipline extends into cell biology. There are reasonable opportunities in private practice.

GENITO-URINARY MEDICINE

The core work of genito-urinary medicine (GUM) relates to sexually transmitted infections. A large part of the work involves the clinical management of patients with HIV infection at all stages of the disease, possibly including in-patient management. The work involves a number of non-infectious medical genital problems such as dermatoses. In recent years it has also expanded into other areas of sexual health, such as the provision of contraception, management of sexual dysfunction, health promotion and colposcopy (for the diagnosis and treatment of cervical dysplasia). HIV medicine is one of the most high-profile, fascinating and rapidly developing fields in the whole of medicine.

GERIATRIC MEDICINE

This is one of the largest branches of general medicine and is concerned with the clinical, preventive, remedial and social aspects of illness of older people. Clinical geriatrics is rapidly becoming both hospital-based and centred in the community. Consultants of the future are increasingly likely to have commitments in both primary and secondary care settings.

INFECTIOUS DISEASES

This specialism includes such activities as: managing emergency hospital admission of a patient suffering from severe infection; managing severe infection in an ITU setting; the management of patients with imported infections (e.g. malaria); the care of immunocompromised patients (including neutropenic and those with HIV infection/AIDS); the management of nosocomial infections, with knowledge of infection control and appropriate liaison with laboratory services.

MEDICAL ONCOLOGY

Medical oncology is a surgical/oncological sub-specialism, which is involved in delivering cytotoxic and biological agents in the management of disease. Although there is very considerable patient contact there is a higher academic potential and profile compared with clinical oncology (radiotherapy and chemotherapy). A recent development in high-dose chemotherapy with stem cell rescue has brought this specialism closer to clinical haematology. There is opportunity for national and international travel to present data at meetings, etc. Most consultants in medical oncology are part of a large team of specialist oncologists within cancer centres.

NEUROLOGY

Neurology is becoming increasingly out-patient based. It remains a very clinical specialism, despite advances in diagnostics, particularly MRI scanning and DNA-based tests. Many conditions are long-standing and there are increasing interactions with rehabilitation. Neuroscience is advancing at a great pace: there have been big advances in therapy and anybody entering the specialism now is bound to deal with the introduction of new treatments for some conditions, such as MS and motor neurone disease, that so far have proven intractable. In addition, the specialism is becoming increasingly involved with acute medical problems, stroke in particular.

NEUROPHYSIOLOGY

Clinical neurophysiology is a branch of the neurosciences concerned with the investigation of neurological disease by techniques that depend on the electrical properties of neural tissue and muscle. It is primarily involved with the diagnosis of nerve entrapments, neuromuscular disease, epilepsy and ophthalmological disease. It increasingly includes the intra-operative monitoring of the integrity of the spinal cord during scoliosis surgery. Other uses include mapping the cortex during epilepsy surgery and localisation of the subthalamic nuclei for surgery for Parkinson's disease and tremor.

NUCLEAR MEDICINE

Nuclear medicine encompasses a wide range of diagnostic and therapeutic clinical procedures using radioactive substances. Common investigations are bone scans for malignancy, ventilation perfusion scans for pulmonary embolus, myocardial perfusion scan and renal studies to investigate relative function and kidney drainage. Radionuclide therapy is also used to target treatment of diseases such as thyrotoxicosis, severe joint inflammation or malignancies. Nuclear medicine posts are daytime jobs, usually with little or no on-call commitment. There are some part-time posts. The majority of posts are in larger teaching hospitals and provide ample patient contact.

OCCUPATIONAL MEDICINE

Occupational medicine specialises in the diagnosis, management and prevention of disease due to, or exacerbated by, workplace factors. It is concerned with all aspects of the effects of work on health and health on work. There are good career opportunities with many large organisations in both manufacturing and service industries with their own in-house occupational health services. Within the NHS, occupational medicine is one of the fastest growing specialisms. The work combines clinical medical practice with the need to influence and shape the behaviour of both individuals and the organisations they work for. It involves visiting workplaces and liasing closely with medical and non-medical colleagues such as occupational hygienists, disability employment advisers, managers and union and safety representatives.

PAEDIATRIC CARDIOLOGY

Paediatric cardiology is concerned with diseases of the heart in the growing and developing individual. Paediatric cardiologists investigate and treat patients with congenital or acquired heart disease, diseases of cardiac rhythm and conduction, and disturbances of cardiac and circulatory function. There are great opportunities for developing clinical and technological skills and for research.

PALLIATIVE MEDICINE

Palliative medicine enables people to make the most of life and eases the distress and difficulties of dying. This specialism is rapidly expanding. It offers opportunities for work in the community, in independent or NHS hospice units and in hospitals. A key feature is working with a skilled multi-professional team with clinical nurse specialists having a relatively autonomous role. Educating others is also a major part of the work. In such a relatively new specialism, a consultant is often involved in the strategy, development and shaping of services.

PUBLIC HEALTH MEDICINE

This deals with the medical aspects of public health practice. Public health physicians tend to deal with the population's health needs rather than those of individual patients. Consultants in public health medicine work with colleagues in other disciplines and undertake many responsibilities. Out-of-hours work is a component of public health medicine practice with regard to the clinical aspects of communicable disease control and environmental health hazard control.

REHABILITATION

Rehabilitation medicine deals with physical disabilities. These may be congenital or acquired from disease or trauma. It is concerned with the management of patients suffering from brain injuries (both traumatic and non-traumatic), spinal cord injury, chronic neurological disease, chronic locomotor disease and amputations (congenital and acquired). It is both a hospital-based and community-based specialisation, treating patients very early on following their injuries, stroke, surgery or disease onset and extending out into the community to ensure that the patient's health, social requirements and leisure needs are met.

RENAL MEDICINE

Nephrology involves the long-term care of patients with a broad range of renal and other disorders. Many types of renal disease have a chronic and often progressive course. For example, a patient may progress to renal failure and require dialysis and subsequently a renal transplant over a period of 10 to 20 years.

RESPIRATORY MEDICINE

Respiratory medicine has links with many other disciplines. Great advances are occurring in our understanding about how the lungs are affected by allergens, pathogens, organisms, occupation, pollution and diet. Disciplines closely linked to respiratory medicine include radiology, microbiology, immunology, oncology and radiotherapy, thoracic surgery, intensive care medicine, occupational medicine and genito-urinary medicine.

RHEUMATOLOGY
This deals with a group of conditions collectively called rheumatic or musculo-skeletal diseases. The term covers over 200 conditions affecting joints, bones, soft tissues and muscles (arthritis and rheumatism are the most frequent self-reported long-standing conditions in Britain).

NHS PAY (2002)
Medical student

- Student in school of medicine. Five-year course plus optional extra year for research study/BSc. In your final year, the tuition fee is paid for you, and you can apply for a means-tested bursary.

Training grades

- Pre-registration house officer (PRHO) in hospital. Basic salary: £18,585. Typical earnings: £30,000.

- Senior House Officer (SHO) working directly with patients as part of a team led by a consultant doctor. Basic salary: £25,000. Typical earnings: £40,000.

GPs

- GP working with a team to provide health care to patients. The majority of GPs are self-employed but a number of salaried options are available. Earnings: £66,280 on average for a full-time self-employed GP.

Hospital doctors

- Specialist Registrar (SpR) working for 4–6 years or longer in a chosen area of special knowledge and expertise. Basic salary: £30,000. Typical earnings: £50,000.

- Consultant, leader of a medical team and responsible for the treatment of patients seen by that team. Basic salary: £52,640. Typical earnings: from £52,640 upwards.

MEDICAL SCHOOLS IN ENGLAND (FIVE-YEAR COURSES):

- University of Birmingham Medical School, Birmingham B15 2TJ. Tel: 0121 414 6888. Website: www.bham.ac.uk.

- Brighton and Sussex Medical School, Mithras House, Lewes Road, Brighton BN2 4AT. Tel: 01273 600900. Website: www.bsms.ac.uk.

- University of Bristol, Senate House, Tyndall Avenue, Bristol BS8 1TH. Tel: 0117 928 7679. Website: www.bris.ac.uk.

- University of Cambridge, Kellet Lodge, Tennis Court Road, Cambridge CB2 1QJ. Tel: 01223 333308. Website: www.cam.ac.uk.

- University of East Anglia, School of Medicine, Health Policy and Practice, Norwich NR4 7TJ. Tel: 01603 593061. Website: www.med.uea.ac.uk.

- Hull York Medical School, Cottingham Road, Hull HU6 7RX. Tel: 01482 466100. Website: www.hyms.ac.uk.

- Keele University, Staffordshire ST5 5BG. Tel: 01782 584005. Website: www.keele.ac.uk.

- University of Leeds, Faculty of Medicine, Leeds LS2 9JT. Tel: 0113 233 4362. Website: www.leeds.ac.uk.

- University of Leicester Medical School, Medical Sciences Building, University Road, Leicester LE1 7RH. Tel: 0116 252 2295. Website: www.le.ac.uk and www.lwms.ac.uk.

- University of Liverpool, Admissions Secretary (Medicine), PO Box 147, 69 3BX. Tel: 0151 709 7172. Website: www.liv.ac.uk.

- University of London: Imperial College School of Medicine, Exhibition Road, South Kensington, London SW7 2AZ. Tel: 020 7594 3598. Website: www.ic.ac.uk.

- University of London: Guy's, King's and St Thomas's Hospitals School of Medicine and Dentistry, Hodgkin Building, Guy's Campus, London SE1 9RT. Tel: 020 7848 6501. Website: www.kcl.ac.uk.

- Queen Mary, University of London, Mile End Road, London E1 4NS. Tel: 020 7882 5555. Website: www.qmul.ac.uk.

- St Bartholomew's and the Royal London School of Medicine and Dentistry, Queen Mary and Westfield College, Turner Street, London E1 2AD. Tel: 020 7377 7611. Website: www.mds.qmw.ac.uk.

- Royal Free and University College London School of Medicine, Rowland Hill Street, London NW3 2PF. Tel: 020 7830 2686. Website: www.ucl.ac.uk.

- St George's Hospital Medical School, Cranmer Terrace, London SW17 ORE. Tel: 020 8672 9944. Website: www.sghms.ac.uk.

- University of Manchester Medical School, Stopford Building, Oxford Road, Manchester M13 9PT. Tel: 0161 275 5025. Website: www.man.ac.uk.

- University of Newcastle upon Tyne, Medical School, Framlington Place, Newcastle upon Tyne NE2 4HH. Tel: 0191 222 7034. Website: www.ncl.ac.uk.

- University of Nottingham Medical School, Queen's Medical Centre, Nottingham NG7 2UH. Tel: 0115 970 9379. Website: www.nott.ac.uk.

- Oxford University Medical School, John Radcliffe Hospital, Headington, Oxford OX3 9DU. Tel: 01865 221689. Website: www.ox.ac.uk.

- Peninsula Medical School (a partnership between the Universities of Exeter and Plymouth and the NHS in Devon and Cornwall), Tamar Science Park, Derriford, Plymouth, Devon PL6 8BX. Tel: 01752 764261. Website: www.pms.ac.uk.

- University of Sheffield Medical School, Beech Hill Road, Sheffield S10 2RX. Tel: 0114 271 2142. Website: www.shef.ac.uk.

- University of Southampton, Biomedical Sciences Building, Ballett Crescent East, Southampton S15 7FX. Tel: 023 8059 4408. Website: www.soton.ac.uk.

- University of Warwick, Coventry CV4 7AL. Tel: 024 7652 3723. Website: www.warwick.ac.uk.

Medical schools in Scotland, Wales and Northern Ireland also offer courses leading to the same qualifications:

- Faculty of Medicine, University of Aberdeen, Regent Walk, Aberdeen AB9 1FX. Tel: 01224 272 090. Website: www.abdn.ac.uk.

- Faculty of Medicine and Dentistry, University of Dundee, Dundee DD1 4HN. Tel: 01382 344160. Website: www.dundee.ac.uk.

- University of Edinburgh Medical School, Edinburgh EH8 9AG. Tel: 0131 650 3187. Website: www.ed.ac.uk.

- Faculty of Medicine, University of Glasgow, Glasgow G12 8QQ. Tel: 0141 330 4424. Website: www.gla.ac.uk.

- The Medical Faculty, Queen's University of Belfast, University Road, Belfast BT7 1NN. Tel: 028 9033 5081. Website: www.qub.ac.uk.

- University of St Andrews, 79 North Street, College Gate, St Andrews KY16 9AJ. Tel: 01334 476161. Website: www.st-and.ac.uk.

- University of Wales College of Medicine, Heath Park, Cardiff CF4 4XN. Tel: 029 2074 2027. Website: www.cf.ac.uk.

Further information: Royal College of Physicians, 11 St Andrew's Place, Regents Park, London NW1 4LE. Tel: 020 7935 1174. Website: www.rcplondon.ac.uk. Email: education@rcplondon.ac.uk.

ENVIRONMENTAL HEALTH OFFICER (EHO)

As an environmental health officer you'll use your specialist skills to develop, co-ordinate and implement public health policies designed to ensure that everyone has the same chance of a better quality of life in a healthier society. There are four important aspects to this work: improving food safety and nutrition; improving housing conditions; improving the environment; and improving workplace health and safety.
There are plenty of areas in which you could work:

● central government and its agencies such as the Food Standards Agency, the Environment Agency and the Health and Safety Executive

● military service

● environmental protection consultancies

● retailers (particularly those concerned with food)

● holiday companies (checking out foreign hotels etc)

● shipping and flight companies (ensuring passengers' on-board health and safety, for example).

Many EHOs work abroad. For example, the European Commission employs some, and others travel further afield to work in Australia, Canada, New Zealand and the USA.

The typical annual salary for a qualified EHO working in a local authority is £20,000 to £30,000. Those promoted to managerial level, or head of department, can expect to receive a salary of up to £60,000 or more. Salaries in the private sector may vary considerably. EHOs working for private companies may earn more than those in local authorities. In addition, many EHOs receive a car allowance for using their private car on official business. Some EHOs have a car provided under a leadership scheme.

To become an EHO in the UK it is necessary to be accepted on a university or college course accredited by the Chartered Institute of Environmental Health. Entry requirements for school leavers include science A levels, an appropriate GNVQ or an equivalent BTEC qualification.

The undergraduate programme (BSc Hons) requires GCSE passes at grade C or better in English language, maths, biology, chemistry and physics, and at least 160 points at AS and A2 level with a science subject at A2 or 200 points at AS and A level without a science subject.

Alternatively, applicants should have a BTEC National Certificate or Diploma in an appropriate science or technology subject with at least five merit passes in subjects at N level or above, or a BTEC Higher National Certificate or Diploma in an appropriate science or technology with at least 6 merit passes in subjects at H level or above. Alternatively, a degree from a UK university in an appropriate science or technology subject or qualifications and experience considered equivalent by the admitting university may be accepted. Exceptionally, applicants without these qualifications may be admitted with prior approval of the CIEH.

Entrants to postgraduate programmes should have at least a lower second class honours degree in a pure or applied science from a UK university, or qualifications and experience considered equivalent by the admitting university. Exceptionally, applicants without these qualifications may be admitted with prior approval of the CIEH.

When you apply to do an accredited course, it is advisable to look for a practical training place as soon as possible. If you can find one before you begin the course, you know you will be able to complete a sandwich route and become qualified in four years (two years if you already have an appropriate science degree and you enrol on an MSc course). If you cannot, you may still be able to enrol on the course, and look for a practical training place while you are a student. If you are unsuccessful in finding a practical training place you can still complete a full-time degree and then, providing it is an accredited full-time course, you can look to obtain your practical training after graduation.

Further information: Chartered Institute of Environmental Health, Chadwick Court, 15 Hatfields, London SE1 8DJ. Tel: 020 7928 6006. Website: www.cieh.org. Email: info@cieh.org.

HAEMATOLOGIST

Haematologists analyse the cellular composition of blood and blood-producing tissues, e.g. bone marrow. The results are used to diagnose patients with anaemia, haemophilia and other genetic disorders, and clotting defects, which are sometimes the result of treatment for other diseases. Haematology in the UK is almost unique in that it spans both the clinical responsibility for looking after patients and active involvement in the haematology laboratory. The specialism is developing rapidly with respect to therapeutic advances and lends itself to research. There is the opportunity to specialise in a wide variety of clinical and laboratory areas, e.g. haemoglobinopathies, haemostasis and thrombosis, transfusion medicine, malignant haematology, etc.

A good degree in one of the biological sciences is the usual entry qualification.

Further information: Recruitment Centre for Clinical Scientists (contact details on p.30).

HEALTH CARE ASSISTANT

Health care assistants work in hospital or community settings under the guidance of a qualified nurse. Duties include washing and dressing, feeding, helping people to mobilise, toileting, bed making, generally assisting with patients' overall comfort, monitoring patients' conditions by taking temperature, pulse, respiration and weight.

There are no national minimum requirements, but you will probably be expected to have a good general education and/or work experience. Health care assistants may have the opportunity to obtain an NVQ qualification in care up to Level 3. Often, obtaining NVQ Level 2 will lead to the person taking on more responsibility. An NVQ Level 3 will meet the minimum entry requirements for entry into nurse training.

Further information: contact the HR/personnel department of your local hospital trust.

HEALTH VISITOR

As a key member of the primary healthcare team, it's your job to promote health in your practice area (most health visitors cover the area of a GP's practice). Health visitors are expected to promote health in the community, including mental, physical and social wellbeing, and they give practical help and advice to the whole family. Some work from doctors' surgeries, while others cover a specific geographical area, visiting people in their homes and schools.

You must be qualified as a registered nurse before you can take a degree programme as a health visitor.

Further information: Nursing and Midwifery Council, 23 Portland Place, London W1B 1PZ. Tel: 020 7637 7181. Website: www.nmc-uk.org; Royal College of Nurses, 20 Cavendish Square, London, W1G 0RN. Tel: 020 7409 3333. Website: www.rcn.org.uk.

HISTOPATHOLOGIST

The main part of the work of a histopathologist is concerned with the microscopic examination of tissues taken as either biopsy samples (e.g. gastric biopsies) or resection specimens (e.g. mastectomy). These tissues are assessed macroscopically and material taken for microscopic examination for the purpose of diagnosis, prognosis and directing appropriate treatment. There is a significant component of cytology, which is the microscopic assessment of preparations of cells as aspirated or obtained from body tissues (e.g. fine needle aspirate of breast, pleural aspirate). Liaison with clinicians via regular patient management meetings is now extensive. Research activities are optional.

Further information: the Royal College of Pathologists produces a booklet, *A Career Guide to Pathology*, Royal College of Pathologists, 2 Carlton House Terrace, London SW1Y 5AF. Tel: 020 7451 6700. Website: www.rcpath.org.

MEDICAL ILLUSTRATOR

Medical illustrators work as part of the healthcare team in all departments in the hospital environment. A medical illustrator may work in studios, clinics, operating theatres or on the wards and is responsible for providing photographic and other visual records of patients and pathological materials. These provide valuable aids to doctors trying to make a diagnosis or confirming effective treatment of disease. Many medical illustrators are becoming involved in specialised techniques such as the use of ultraviolet and infrared light photography. They are also involved in providing a wide range of graphics services such as audio-visual teaching and lecture material and artwork for scientific posters, brochures and other medical publications.

Applicants will require a media qualification in photography, graphic design or video to be eligible for training. There is also an accreditation scheme for those who do not have the necessary qualifications. Training is by a three-year in-service training programme leading to a BSc in medical illustration from Glasgow Caledonian University. It is also possible to study for the degree full time, with work placements in the final year. Applicants with a relevant first degree and working in a recognised medical illustration department can take a one-year distance-learning course.

Further information: Institute of Medical Illustrators, Medical and Dental Illustration Unit, Leeds Dental Institute, Clarendon Way, Leeds, West Yorkshire LS2 9LU.

MEDICAL LABORATORY ASSISTANT (MLA)

Many of the skills an MLA learns can be used to support any aspect of pathology – clinical chemistry, haematology, transfusion science, cytopathology, histopathology, medical microbiology, immunology or tissue typing. As an MLA, you can work on receiving, sorting and labelling tissue samples; recording laboratory data; sterilising and disinfecting equipment; disposal of chemical or biological waste; making up solutions of chemicals or growth media; maintaining stocks of reagents and consumable items; phlebotomy; separation of blood serum and plasma.

MLA Pay (April 2002)

MLA/ATO*	£9,300–£12,900
Senior ATO*	£11,500–£15,100
Trainee cytology screeners	£10,100–£10,500
Cytology screeners	£12,000–£17,700

*Assistant Technical Officer

No formal educational or age requirements, although you may need to pass four (or more) GCSEs (or equivalent) to qualify for some more advanced work. As an MLA you will be trained first in how to work safely in the laboratory and to understand how your job is part of the hospital's day-to-day work. Then you will be given more specialised individual training.

Further information: Institute of Biomedical Science (contact details on p. 41).

MEDICAL LABORATORY SCIENTIFIC OFFICER (MLSO)

The work is mainly laboratory-based with the opportunity to work in a range of subjects including clinical chemistry, haematology, histopathology, medical microbiology, transfusion science, virology, cytopathology, virology, histology and immunology. Along with other biomedical scientists, MLSOs work mainly in hospitals, in the Blood Transfusion Service and the Public Health Laboratory Service. Some may also be employed in specialised university research departments. In a wide range of laboratories, both manual and automated methods of analysis are used, though today computerised data processing and information retrieval systems are common.

NHS PAY
The following information should be used only as guidance, as pay can vary between individual NHS trusts and laboratories:

Trainee MLSO

This is the grade on which people complete in-service training having obtained, or while studying for, their CPSM-approved degree (Council for Professions Supplementary to Medicine now replaced by the Health Professions Council, www.hpc-uk.org)
Salary: £11,500–£12,900.

MLSO 1

Newly qualified grade, which involves the performance of basic laboratory work. More experienced officers may take charge of a section of work or supervise unqualified staff.
Salary: £15,700–£21,600.

MLSO 2

Staff performing complex laboratory work requiring particular initiative, or in technical charge of smaller departments. They will usually be required to have gained higher level qualifications such as Fellowship of the Institute of Biomedical Science (IBMS).
Salary: £19,900–£28,400.

MLSO 3

Those involved in highly skilled individual work on complex examinations or those who take technical charge of the operations of a larger department will usually be on this grade.
Salary: £25,200–£31,900.

MLSO 4

Usually in overall technical charge of organising the work of a group of pathology departments or a large department, or make major individual contributions that involve the application and/or development of specialised techniques. They may also work in higher levels of pathology management. Salary: £29,500–£37,400.

There are three routes of entry: by acquiring a BSc honours degree in biomedical science; through possession of another relevant degree; or with life science A levels (or possibly GNVQs), in which case you will then have to find an employer who is prepared to allow you time off to study part-time on a relevant degree course. In all cases of direct entry, for the purposes of state registration, you will need to get written confirmation from the Health Professions Council (HPC) about the acceptability of any degree you hold or intend studying for. If you are already a graduate with a degree that has been accepted by HPC, you may find more posts are available to you as your training period will be shorter. Vacancies are advertised in the local or national press and in various specialist journals. If you wish to be employed direct from school or college, you may possibly be able to find a trainee post. However, you would also need to secure a university place.

Further information: Institute of Biomedical Science (contact details on p. 41).

MEDICAL MICROBIOLOGY AND VIROLOGY

Medical microbiology is a laboratory-based specialism dealing with the diagnosis, management and control of infection. Medical virology is a sub-specialism that deals with viral disease alone. Although both involve a laboratory component, they also require clinical judgement and collaboration with colleagues, frequently at the bedside. Aside from dealing with patients, the environment is important in microbiological practice: the design and maintenance of operating theatres and other clinical areas, food preparation and hygiene, cleaning and waste disposal, sterilisation and disinfection.

Two years' general training is required. Trainees may enter the SpR grade after having gained a year's experience in microbiology/virology as an SHO or by acquiring suitable training in general medicine. Those who have undergone training in general medicine without experience of microbiology/virology should normally have obtained the MRCP (UK). During this period of training, it is expected that not less than six months' experience would have been gained in one or more of the following: infectious diseases, genito-urinary medicine (including HIV), paediatrics, oncology, transplantation medicine, chest medicine. Increasing competition for SpR posts has resulted in successful applicants having extensive experience in general medicine, a laboratory specialisation, or a higher degree (MSc, MD, PhD).

Further information: Royal College of Pathologists (contact details on p. 63).

MEDICAL PHYSICIST

Medical physicists apply physical sciences to the diagnosis and treatment of disease, and to maintain the safety of patients and of other health care workers. Many medical physicists work in ionising radiation science. Physicists develop systems for image capture, image processing and quality assurance, to optimise the diagnostic use of X- and X-gamma-radiation. They plan complex treatments for individual patients, develop planning methods and manage quality assurance programmes in radiotherapy. Physicists provide radiation protection advice and services in hospitals. Mathematical modelling of pressure, temperature, flow and perfusion, and the design of transducers and electronic systems, is a growing field. You will need to keep abreast of scientific and medical research in your own area, and to develop your own laboratory, computational and management skills. Most medical physicists are based in large hospitals with a number of other specialist physicists, engineers and technical staff. They usually provide a service or advice to a group of nearby hospitals.

The minimum qualification is normally an honours degree in physical or engineering science. A higher degree or industrial experience may be valuable.

Further information: Institution of Physics and Engineering in Medicine, Fairmount House, 230 Tadcaster Road, York YO24 1ES. Tel: 01904 610821. Email: office@ipem.org.uk. Website: www.ipem.org.uk.

MEDICAL TECHNICIAN

Hospitals use an increasingly wide range of complex, specialised equipment to diagnose illness, treat patients and monitor the results of treatment. Cutting-edge technology is used in areas including radiotherapy, bioengineering, dialysis, laser procedures, magnetic resonance imaging and ultrasound. Medical technicians are responsible for maintaining and servicing such equipment. They also check its performance, sometimes operate it, and gauge any environmental effects.

Although there are no minimum entry qualifications, employing authorities will usually expect qualifications acceptable for college or university – either four GCSEs (grade C or above) or a science A Level or a BTEC National Award in electronics – or a degree in engineering.

Further information: Institute of Physics and Engineering in Medicine (contact details above).

MIDWIFE

As a midwife you will have the lead professional role in preparing for and managing deliveries, intervening where necessary and knowing what to do if the mother or baby is sick. Midwives have a client group who are on the whole very healthy, and in need of help and advice only because they are expecting a baby. The birth itself may be at the heart of the process, but midwives provide support to women, their babies, their partners and families, from conception to the first phase of post-natal care. As your experience grows you can research and develop special areas of practice, become involved in services such as family planning, or move into teaching or management. See pay scale on p. 72.

I first trained as a midwife 25 years ago after completing a three-year nursing training in England. After working as a midwife for a short time, I gave up work for 10 years to have my two children. Both births were home births and I am a strong advocate of planned home births. Three years ago I set up a consultant's room from home and now manage up to 36 clients, equating to around three births a month. Usually I see a woman around six to 12 weeks into the pregnancy, then every four to six weeks until the pregnancy reaches 30 to 32 weeks. From then on I will see the woman fortnightly until the pregnancy is at the 36-week mark and then the visits continue weekly until the baby is born. I have delivered at least 200 babies since becoming an independent midwife 12 years ago.

Marion, Midwife

Normal minimum age of entry is 17½, with five GCSE passes or equivalent at grade C or above including English language or literature and a science subject. Apply via the Nursing and Midwifery Admissions Service (see below). You can also do a shortened midwifery course after qualifying as a registered nurse.

Further information:

● Nursing and Midwifery Admissions Service (NMAS), Rosehill, New Barn Lane, Cheltenham, Gloucestershire GL52 3LZ. Tel: 01242 544949 (general enquiries); 01242 223707 (application materials). Website: www.nmas.ac.uk

● Nursing and Midwifery Council (see p. 62).

● Royal College of Midwives, Royal College of Midwives, 15 Mansfield Street, London W1G 9NH. Tel: 020 7312 3535. Website: www.rcm.org.uk.

MOLECULAR GENETICIST

Molecular genetics uses chemical examination of cellular DNA to define genetic abnormalities. The bulk of the work falls into three categories: prenatal diagnosis in families in which single gene disorders have been identified by DNA analysis; carrier testing and risk assessment for identifying presymptomatic individuals at risk for single gene disorders; confirmation of diagnosis for genetic disorders. The laboratory genetics service is mainly organised on a regional basis, and the scientists work in hospital laboratories. They work closely with a wide range of professionals including medical staff and genetic counsellors.

Graduates in genetics or a variety of life sciences are eligible for entry into the Grade A training programme. Some candidates obtain a higher degree before entry.

Further information: Recruitment Centre for Clinical Scientists (contact details on p. 30).

NURSE

ADULT

Your place of work may be a hospital ward or specialist clinic, or it could be out in the community, visiting people at home or attached to local health centres. Nurses are also at the forefront of highly specialist areas such as intensive care, theatre and recovery, cancer care and care of the elderly.

When it comes to career prospects, you can't beat it.
Lisa, Staff Nurse, Cardiac Unit

CHILDREN

Children's nursing can take you from intensive care of a newborn baby with breathing problems to looking after a six-foot-tall adolescent whose leg has been broken in a soccer match. Children's nurses work closely with patients' families as part of the caring process.

CONSULTANT POSTS FOR NURSES, MIDWIVES AND HEALTH VISITORS (A NEW INITIATIVE)

Post holders will spend a minimum of 50 per cent of their time working directly with patients, ensuring that people using the NHS continue to benefit from the very best nursing and midwifery skills. They will also be responsible for developing personal practice, being involved in research and evaluation and contributing to education, training and development. Nurse consultants will be placed on a salary scale in the range of £24,460 to £42,010.

DISTRICT NURSE

District nursing teams work in partnership with patients and their carers, primary and secondary care colleagues, social services, voluntary agencies and many others to assess healthcare needs and develop appropriate packages of care. Clinical care includes:

- identifying the physical, emotional and social needs of people in a range of community settings and identifying the wider needs of the community

- preparing comprehensive packages of care for people with acute, chronic or terminal illness

- control of pain and other symptoms

- prescribing suitable treatments from the nurses' formulary

- technical care, such as intravenous therapy administration

- assessment, diagnosis and treatment of patients with tissue viability needs

- support and education of carers in their caring role

- planning rehabilitation programmes with patients, families and other professionals

- promotion of health and self-help care.

LEARNING DISABILITY

The role of this nurse is to help people with a learning disability to maintain and improve their lifestyles, and to participate fully as equal members of society. You will be working in a wide variety of settings: people's own homes, their family homes, residential care, schools, workplaces and leisure. As your career unfolds you can maintain this broad spread of activity or specialise in an area such as sensory disability, education, or management of learning disability services.

MENTAL HEALTH

At any one time, one adult in six suffers from some form of mental illness. In recent years, there has been a significant shift from hospitals to the community as the setting for mental health care. Nurses work in people's homes, in small residential units and in local health centres, with considerable autonomy in how they plan and deliver care. As a mental health nurse you are likely to be dealing with people of all ages and from a wide range of backgrounds. As your career develops you may choose to specialise in areas such as drugs and alcohol misuse or working with offenders. You could also become involved in education, research, or management roles. Mental health nurses are also the most likely to be responsible for co-ordinating a patient's care in the community.

NATIONAL BLOOD SERVICE

The demand for blood, increasing commitments in tissue banking and meeting the changing needs of the NHS mean there are a variety of career opportunities in working for the National Blood Service.

Further information: National Nurse Advisor, National Blood Authority, Oak House, Reeds Crescent, Watford, Hertfordshire WD1 1QH. Tel: 01923 486800.

NHS Nursing and midwifery pay scales

Grade	Min (£)	Max (£)	Pay rates in Inner London Min (£)	Max (£)
Grade A	9,735	12,220	12,963	15,448
Grade B	11,455	13,485	14,683	16,713
Grade C	13,040	16,005	16,790	19,873
Grade D	16,005	17,670	19,873	21,605
Grade E	17,105	20,655	21,017	24,709
Grade F	18,970	23,690	22,956	27,865
Grade F	*24,125*	*24,565*	*28,318*	*28,775*
Grade G	22,385	26,340	26,508	30,568
Grade G	*26,790*	*27,245*	*31,018*	*31,473*
Grade H	25,005	29,065	29,233	33,293
Grade H	*29,525*	*29,990*	*33,753*	*34,218*
Grade H Modern Matron	25,005	29,990	29,233	34,218
Grade I	27,695	31,830	31,923	36,058
Grade I	*32,295*	*32,760*	*36,523*	*36,988*
Grade I Modern Matron	27,695	32,760	31,923	36,988

Text in italics refers to discretionary points

Other nursing roles include: nursery nurse, play specialist and in-flight nurse.

Normal minimum age of entry is 17 with five GCSE passes or equivalent at grade C or above including English language or literature and a science subject.

Further information: Nursing and Midwifery Council (contact details on p. 62); Royal College of Nurses (contact details on p. 69); Nursing and Midwifery Admissions Service (contact details on p. 69).

OBSTETRICS AND GYNAECOLOGY

Obstetrics and gynaecology comprises the care of the pregnant woman, her unborn child and the management of diseases specific to women. Most consultants are generalists; there are a number of sub-specialisms, which include materno-foetal medicine, gynaecological oncology, gynaecological urology, reproductive medicine and community gynaecology. The surgical work is varied and involves close co-operation with other specialisms such as urology, colorectal surgery and oncology. The medical aspects of the work involve liaison with endocrinologists, renal physicians and cardiologists.

Under a programme prepared by the Royal College of Obstetricians and Gynaecologists (RCOG), the minimum length of training will be six or seven years from the time of full registration with the General Medical Council. The training programme incorporates supervision, guidance, continuous assessment and optimal learning opportunities. During this time the college's membership examination must be passed (MRCOG), after which trainees are encouraged to obtain some specialist experience in foetal medicine, reproductive medicine, gynaecological oncology or uro-gynaecology. When the programme is completed satisfactorily, and with the approval of the regional Postgraduate Dean, the RCOG recommends that the General Medical Council grant the certificate of completion of specialist training (CCST). The doctor is then eligible to be added to the RCOG's list of those participating in the programme of continuing medical education (CME) and personal development.

Trainees wishing to work part-time may do so through flexible training posts funded by regional Postgraduate Deans or by job sharing. Some may wish to take up a full-time appointment in due course and some may continue to seek part-time appointments as consultants, associate specialists or staff grade doctors. Job sharing posts are arranged by individual trusts or departments but the RCOG has an adviser in flexible training who maintains a job-share register and from whom more details are available.

Further information: Royal College of Obstetricians and Gynaecologists, 27 Sussex Place, London NW1 4RG. Tel: 020 7772

6200. Website: www.rcog.org.uk. For careers advice at the RCOG, email cwood@rcog.org.uk.

OCCUPATIONAL THERAPY

OCCUPATIONAL THERAPIST
Occupational therapists help people overcome physical, psychological or social problems arising from illness or disability by concentrating on what they are able to achieve rather than on their disabilities. Demand for occupational therapists in health and social services is strong and growing. The NHS offers rotational posts, which gives you the chance to work in a range of areas, or you can work specifically in an area of your choice.

Normally five GCSE passes and at least two, often three, A levels, or equivalent, including one in a science subject, are required for entry to a degree course.

I have variety in my daily activities, such as working alongside elderly people, helping people to become independent in the community, aiding clients to relearn self-care skills and helping people to use new equipment to improve the quality of their life.
Sonia, Senior Occupational Therapist with both clinical and management roles

REHABILITATION ASSISTANT/TECHNICAL INSTRUCTOR
This can sometimes be a route to an in-service degree course leading to an occupational therapist. You may need to pass four (or more) GCSEs (or equivalent) to qualify for some more advanced work. A mature approach is essential. Contact your local NHS employer to see what opportunities are available in your local area; or Universities and Colleges Admission Service (UCAS).

NHS Pay (April 2002)

Helpers	£10,080–£12,800
Occupational therapist (newly qualified)	£17,100–£19,100
Senior II	£18,300–£23,400

Senior I and Head IV   £21,800–£26,000
Head III   £24,900–£27,600
Consultant   £33,900–£46,600
Further information: College of Occupational Therapists, 106–114
Borough High Street, London SE1 1LB. Tel: 020 7357 6480; careers
hotline: 020 7450 2332. Email: anne.fenech@cot.co.uk. Websites:
www.cot.org.uk/ wwwcot.co.uk, and www.baot.org.uk/
www.baot.co.uk.

OPHTHALMOLOGY

Ophthalmology is the medical and surgical management of
conditions of the eye and its adenexa. The speciality covers all age
ranges. A new speciality of purely medical ophthalmology is now
developing. Ophthalmology involves the care of eye conditions in
patients of all ages from premature neonates right through to the
elderly. The range of conditions encountered in ophthalmology is
wide – trauma, cataracts, diabetic eye disease, congenital and
genetic eye problems. The opportunity for sub-specialisation is
equally wide. A range of skills, both medical and surgical, is
required for ophthalmology. There are opportunities for an
academic or laboratory based career.

Further information: Royal College of Ophthalmologists,
17 Cornwall Terrace, London NW1 4QW. Tel: 0207 935 0702.
Website: www.rcophth.ac.uk

ORTHOPTIST

Orthoptists investigate and diagnose a range of eye problems and
determine the best way to manage them. This might involve
prescribing eye exercises or referring the patient for special
spectacle lenses or for eye surgery. They use special equipment to
measure the pressure inside the eye, to assess the patient's field
of vision and to carry out other testing procedures. In some
clinics, orthoptists work with ophthalmologists in helping to
manage conditions such as glaucoma.

NHS Pay (from April 2002)
Orthoptist   £17,100–£19,100
Senior II   £18,300–£23,400

Senior I and Head IV	£21,800–£26,000
Head III	£24,900–£27,600
Head II	£27,140–£30,970
Head I	£30,970–£34,190
Consultant	£33,940–£46,600

I work mainly with children in diagnosis and helping to correct their vision but I also work with adults who have vision problems due to an accident. The research work I do is in connection with treatment outcomes.

John, Research Orthoptist with an eye hospital

Usually five GCSEs, or equivalent, including English, maths and at least one science, plus three A levels or equivalent. Mature applicants are considered on an individual basis.

Further information: British Orthoptic Society, Tavistock House North, Tavistock Square, London WC1H 9HX. Tel: 020 7387 7992. Email: bos@orthoptics.org.uk. Website: www.orthoptics.org.uk.

ORTHOTIST

Orthotists often work in out-patient clinics. Their patients include older people needing special shoes because of arthritis, children with cerebral palsy needing individually designed splints and people with back problems needing a special brace. The orthotist assesses the patient's problem and decides upon a prescription. He or she then designs the orthosis, supervises its manufacture, fitting and adjustment, and teaches the patient how to use it.

Three A levels or equivalent with good grades, including maths and at least one science, preferably physics, chemistry or biology. Mature students without the necessary qualifications will be considered.

Further information: British Association of Prosthetists and Orthotists, Sir James Clark Building, Abbey Mill Business Centre,

Paisley PA1 1TJ. Tel: 0141 561 7217. Email: admin@bapo.com. Website: www.bapo.com.

OSTEOPATHY

Osteopaths work on the neuromusculoskeletal system, primarily muscles and joints. An important principle of osteopathy is that the body is a unit, acknowledging that the neuromusculoskeletal system can affect and is affected by internal organs. The osteopath is particularly interested in those mechanical and structural factors that have predisposed the person to and maintained the person's symptoms, which may be in another part of the body entirely. An osteopath may use a wide range of manual techniques as part of treatment. In addition, patient management may involve advice on exercise, posture or diet.

If you would like to become an osteopath, you will need to study at a school recognised by the General Osteopathic Council. Providers of osteopathic education offer a number of different opportunities to study for a degree in osteopathy. Some provide mixed-mode time training over five years, others full-time over four years and some a combination of the two. Some institutions also provide courses leading to postgraduate awards including higher degrees, such as MSc. The majority of institutions currently offering osteopathic education are located in the south of England, where osteopathy has a long history of independent provision. Some universities intend to provide osteopathic education within the university campus setting as part of their portfolio of health care education courses.

Accredited institutions providing osteopathic education in the UK:

- British College of Osteopathic Medicine, 3 Sumpter Close, 120–122 Finchley Road, London, NW3 5HR. Tel: 020 7435 6464. Website: www.bcom.ac.uk.

- British School of Osteopathy, 275 Borough High Street, London, SE1 1JE. Tel: 020 7407 0222. Website: www.bso.ac.uk.

- College of Osteopaths Educational Trust, 13 Furzehill Road, Borehamwood, Hertfordshire WD6 2DG. Tel: 020 8905 1937. Website: www.collegeofosteopaths.ac.uk.

- European School of Osteopathy, Boxley House, The Street, Boxley, Near Maidstone, Kent, ME14 3GZ. Tel: 01622 671558. Website: www.eso.ac.uk.

- London School of Osteopathy, First Floor, 56–60 Nelson Street, London, E1 2DE. Tel: 020 7265 9333. Website: www.londonschoolofosteopathy.com.

Further information: General Osteopathic Council, Premier House, 10 Greycoat Place, Victoria, London SW1P 1SB. Tel: 020 7357 6655. Website: www.osteopathy.org.uk.

PAEDIATRICIAN

Paediatrics is a holistic specialty that focuses on the child within a family, working to minimise the adverse effect of disease and to allow children to live as normal a life as possible. There are opportunities to develop skills in specialty areas including community paediatrics and neonatal intensive care. General paediatrics remains the bedrock of the service, but there are opportunities to develop close links with primary care, child and adolescent psychiatry and public health, as well as other medical specialties (e.g. diabetes, cystic fibrosis and epilepsy).

General professional training usually begins after completion of pre-registration hospital posts. The responsibility for approval of posts for general professional training in paediatrics in England, Wales and Northern Ireland is jointly held by the Royal College of Paediatrics and Child Health and the Royal College of General Practitioners.

Further information: Royal College of Paediatrics and Child Health, 50 Hallam Street, London W1N 6DE. Tel: 020 7307 5600. Email: enquiries@rcpch.ac.uk. Website: www.rcpch.ac.uk. Head of Education and Training: Rosalind Topping (email: rosalind.topping@rcpch.ac.uk).

PARAMEDIC

Paramedics treat and stabilise patients at the scene of their accident or illness, while ensuring that they get to hospital as quickly as possible. Applicants will need to be a minimum of 18 years old, be physically fit, and hold a clean driving licence.

Entrants must pass a medical examination and many services conduct a police check on staff who will have substantial access to children. Paramedics can earn around £18,800 with the NHS.

In England, requirements differ between local ambulance services but may include GCSEs or alternative qualifications.

The thing that keeps you going is knowing that you make a difference. There are at least a dozen people alive today who had cardiac arrests and whom I resuscitated at the scene. I've kept in touch with some of them.

Alan, Paramedic

Ambulance technician/care assistant: no formal educational or age requirements, although you may need to pass four (or more) GCSEs (or equivalent) to qualify for some more advanced work.

Further information: Ambulance Service Association, Friars House, 157–168 Blackfriars Road, London SE1 8EU. Tel: 020 7928 9620. Email: office@bizuk.com. Website: www.asa.uk.net.

PATHOLOGIST

Pathologists specialise in the detection of disease through the use of a variety of investigative techniques. Their work can be vital in finding an accurate and early diagnosis, improving the prospects for treatment, identifying sources of disease and reducing the risk of further spread. Chemical pathology/clinical biochemistry involves the study and investigation of the biochemical basis of disease processes with particular emphasis on metabolic diseases. Consultants are involved in organising the laboratory aspects of the biochemistry service and in the future a sub-specialism designation (metabolic medicine) will identify that they have a particular role in the management of patients with metabolic disease, including diabetes, bone disease, inborn errors and lipid disorders. The discipline involves an integration of laboratory and clinical medicine with good opportunities to participate in clinical research.

There are three ways in which you can work in pathology: as a medically qualified doctor, as a clinical scientist or as a biomedical scientist. Each has a different and essential role and requires different qualifications and training. Specialist training following medical qualification typically takes at least six years, although many trainee pathologists take time out from their training (two to three years) to do a research degree. Training takes place in the context of paid employment from the time of qualification onwards.

Further information: Royal College of Pathologists (contact details on p. 63).

PHARMACIST

HOSPITAL PHARMACIST

As the medicines expert, you are the person who should be most aware of adverse effects that a medicine or combination of medicines may produce. You will also give advice on dosage, suggest the most appropriate form of medication and discuss with the medical staff the problems patients may experience with their medicines. You will be expected to provide advice on medicines for individual patients, especially those with heart failure, kidney or liver disease, and for pregnant or breast-feeding women who should not take certain medicines. You will use the Internet and worldwide databases extensively when answering drug queries from medical and nursing staff and from patients. You will also use computers for dispensing, stock control, therapeutic drug monitoring and audit. You will validate prescriptions, check the dose, make sure it is the right drug for the patient and her or his condition, and look for interactions between different medicines.

Entry to the profession is through a four-year pharmacy degree course followed by one year's competence-based, pre-registration training and a registration examination. For the degree course, you need three A level passes (or equivalent): one in chemistry and two others from biology, mathematics or physics, as well as GCSEs (or equivalent) in English language and maths.

HOSPITAL PHARMACY TECHNICIAN

There are no minimum entry requirements, although employers and colleges will normally expect four GSCEs at A, B, or C (or equivalent) usually including science, maths and English. Employers may accept qualifications from mature entrants or from pharmacy assistants and provide additional training and learning.

Pharmacy is discovering itself and there is lots of variety in the work. The profession has lots of challenges facing it and is expanding all the time.
Noel, working in his own pharmacy attached to the University of Stirling campus

Further information: contact the HR/personnel department or chief pharmacist at your local hospital.

Hospital Pharmacists' Pay (April 2002)

Pre-registration graduates	£12,900
Grade A	£18,100–£20,400
Grade B	£20,400–£22,900
Grade C	£22,900–£29,800
Grade D	£28,700–£34,400
Grade E	£32,300–£38,600
Grade F	£36,500–£42,800
Grade G	£40,700–£47,000
Grade H	£47,000–£52,200

COMMUNITY PHARMACIST
Community pharmacists, working from high-street, local and rural pharmacies, use their detailed knowledge to ensure that medicines ordered on doctors' prescriptions or bought over the counter are correctly and safely supplied, with appropriate patient counselling on use, adverse side effects, etc. They also act as readily accessible health advisors to the general public.

Further information: Royal Pharmaceutical Society of Great Britain, 1 Lambeth High Street, London SE1 7JN. Tel: 020 7735 9141. Email: enquiries@rpsgb.org.uk. Website: www.rpsgb.org.uk.

PHLEBOTOMIST

Phlebotomists must take blood without harming the patient. If the patient is in hospital, you will have to make sure that you collect their blood without disturbing their nursing care. You also need to make sure that the specimen of blood is unharmed, or the test results might be either unobtainable or worthless. Once you have taken the specimen, your next job is to label it accurately and deliver it promptly and safely to the right laboratory. Many phlebotomists work part-time, but others combine the work with other duties as an MLA within the laboratory.

No formal educational or age requirements, although you may need to pass four (or more) GCSEs (or equivalent) to qualify for some more advanced work.

Further information: Institute of Biomedical Science (contact details on p. 41).

PHYSIOTHERAPIST

Patients are normally referred to a physiotherapist by a doctor, but some physiotherapists in private practice have patients who are self-referred. The physiotherapist assesses them and decides upon the most appropriate treatment, which might involve exercise, movement, hydrotherapy, electrotherapy and techniques such as massage and manipulation. Physiotherapists play a large role in rehabilitating people after illness or accidents. Health education, aimed at preventing disease and injury, is also an important part of the work.

NHS Pay (April 2002)
Helpers under supervision
Aged 18	£10,00–£12,000
With relevant NVQ Level 2	£12,480
With relevant NVQ Level 3	£12,850

Physiotherapist
With 3 years' training	£17,100–£19,155
Graduate with 4 years' training	£17,700–£19,115

Senior II	£18,300–£23,400
Senior I	£21,800–£26,000
Superintendent IV	£24,900–£27,600
Superintendent III	£24,900–£27,600
Superintendent II	£27,100–£29,990
Superintendent I	£29,900–£33,000
District II	£33,000–£36,500
District I	£36,530–£37,800

You need five GCSEs, including at least two sciences, and a minimum of three A levels, or equivalent qualifications.

Further information: Chartered Society of Physiotherapy, 14 Bedford Row, London WC1R 4ED. Tel: 020 7306 6666. Email: careersadviser@csphysio.org.uk. Website: www.csp.org.uk.

PODIATRIST

Podiatrists offer foot treatment to all age groups, ranging from simple nail care to minor nail surgery, from mechanical correction of gait and posture to invasive surgical techniques. Following graduation, the podiatrist may pursue one or more particular clinical interests. General podiatry involves the regular palliative treatment of the foot, dealing with corns and calluses, in-growing toenails, verrucae and minor skin afflictions. Biomechanics applies engineering principles to the lower limb in order to understand and treat a number of conditions, which result in dysfunction. Diabetic care presents a significant level of risk owing to poor circulation and reduced sensation. Appropriate intervention can reduce the risk of ulceration or amputation. In arthritis the foot is often misshapen, stiff and functionally impaired. The use of modified footwear and insoles can reduce the effects of trauma to the foot. Podiatric surgeons perform surgical correction of a wide range of foot problems and deformities.

NHS Pay
Footcare assistants	£10,000–£12,000
with relevant NVQ Level 2	£12,480
with relevant NVQ Level 3	£12,850
Chiropodist/Podiatrist	£17,100–£19,100

Sen II	£18,300–£23,400
Sen I and Chief IV	£21,800–£26,000
Chief III	£24,900–£27,600
District Chief II	£29,000–£29,990
District Chief I	£31,990–£35,360
District Senior Chief	£33,000–£36,530

There are fourteen recognised schools of podiatry, all departments of universities or colleges of higher education. They award BSc/BSc (Hons) degrees in podiatry, which are recognised for state registration, essential for employment within the NHS. Each school operates its own admissions policy, but in general, two A level passes (to include at least one science) are needed, plus at least five GCSEs (or equivalent) including English, maths and at least one science subject, preferably biology. Alternative qualifications are science access, Advanced GNVQ (merit) and BTEC (usually supported by a science A level) in appropriate subjects. In Scotland, three passes at H level (one B and two Cs with one pass in a science subject).

Podiatry has a good record of accepting mature students, who should be able to support their application with relevant work experience or other qualifications. Applicants will need to complete a health questionnaire to ensure their fitness for clinical practice. This includes a requirement to be immunised against Hepatitis B. In addition, disclosure of any criminal record will be required, as podiatrists work with children and other vulnerable groups.

After graduation there are opportunities for postgraduate research leading to master's degrees and doctorates. The Society of Chiropodists and Podiatrists has its own fellowship examination in general podiatry or in surgery. A teacher's certificate is also obtainable.

Further information: Society of Chiropodists and Podiatrists, 1 Fellmonger's Path, Tower Bridge Road, London SE1 3LY. Tel: 020 7234 8620. Email: enq@scpod.org. Website: www.feetforlife.org.

PROSTHETIST

Prosthetists design a replacement limb by taking a plaster cast of the area on to which it is to fit and modelling it to ensure it will be safe and comfortable. They supervise the technicians assembling the prosthesis and then fit it and advise patients on how to use it. Starting salaries can be between £17,500 and £22,000.

Three A levels with good grades, including maths and at least one science, preferably physics, chemistry or biology, or equivalent. Mature students without the necessary qualifications will be considered.

Further information: British Association of Prosthetists and Orthotists (contact details on p. 76).

PSYCHOLOGICAL THERAPIES

PSYCHOLOGIST

Psychologists bring psychological theory and practice to bear on solving problems or bringing about improvements for individuals, groups and organisations. The NHS employs psychologists in four main specialisms: clinical work, counselling, forensic work and health psychology. Psychologists can specialise in various areas, including mental health work and educational and occupational psychology. There are separate postgraduate training routes for the four branches of applied psychology. The NHS funds a certain number of training places for clinical psychologists.

NHS Pay (April 2002)

Assistant psychologist	£12,040–£14,090
Trainee clinical psychologist	£14,650–£16,480
Clinical psychologist Grade A	£16,480–£37,560
Clinical psychologist Grade B	£36,120–£60,140

An honours degree in psychology, or equivalent, recognised by the British Psychological Society. Contact Clearing House for Postgraduate Courses in Clinical Psychology, University of Leeds, 15 Hyde Terrace, Leeds LS2 9LT.
Website: www.leeds.ac.uk/chpccp. For counselling and health psychology courses, contact the British Psychological Society.

If sports psychology is chosen as a career, there are at least three paths, largely part-time, that lead from a degree to work in sports psychology. The first is teaching and research in sport science within a university, alongside providing a sport psychology service for university athletes. Second, there is teaching and research in psychology while consulting with individual athletes and teams in one's own time. Finally, there is full time consulting with athletes, presently for just a few practitioners of whom some may have specialist clinical or counselling qualifications.

Dr Ian Cockerill, Chair, BPS Sport and Exercise Psychology Section

PSYCHIATRIST

Psychiatrists deal with mental health. They often combine a broad general caseload alongside an area of special expertise and research. There are a number of sub-specialisms within psychiatry, each requiring its own Certificate of Completion of Specialist Training (CCST).

- Child and adolescent psychiatry (CAP) deals with the diagnosis and management of psychiatric disorders from infancy to mid-teens.

- Forensic psychiatry focuses on the assessment and treatment of mentally disordered offenders, and other patients presenting with severe mental disorder in association with significant behavioural disturbance. Treatment settings range from high-security hospitals to medium secure units and community forensic services to prisons.

- General psychiatry encompasses the management of patients in hospital and community settings and may involve working with patients in one of the sub-specialtisms of general psychiatry, such as rehabilitation, substance misuse or liaison psychiatry.

- Learning disability is a sub-specialism of psychiatry, dealing with the assessment and treatment of emotional, behavioural and psychiatric disorder associated with learning disability. Practitioners also provide advice and education about behavioural aspects of learning disability to parents and other carers and to other professionals such as teachers. Much work is done in settings other than hospitals (clinics, day centres, family homes, community group homes) and the psychiatric contribution to multi-disciplinary working is greatly valued. There is great scope for research.

- Old age psychiatry provides a service to all elderly people suffering from organic illness (e.g. dementias of various types), or functional illness (e.g. depression, schizophrenia, etc.).

Specialist psychotherapy is an important part of all psychiatric services, but there is increasing interest in applying psychotherapeutic principles in other settings, such as psychiatric liaison, forensic centres, in the community and in general practice. In the past, much psychotherapy was psychodynamic (using the therapeutic relationship and helping the patient explore their current problems in the light of past relationships). Now there is more emphasis on the trainee having a wider view, which includes cognitive-behavioural (concerned with learned patterns of thought and ways of modifying them) and systemic work (understanding the system in which a patient has difficulties, e.g. the family or couple). A wide range of patients is referred to psychotherapy services, with the emphasis currently (as with much of psychiatry) being on those with more serious mental illness, especially personality disorder and co-morbid conditions. Work is usually arranged within strict time boundaries, so the specialism is ideal for those who work part time.

NHS Pay (April 2002)

Assistant child psychotherapist	£15,100–£16,400
Trainee child psychotherapist	£17,000–£20,700
Child psychotherapist Grade A	£20,700–£38,900
Child psychotherapist Grade B	£37,400–£62,300

Further information: Royal College of Psychiatrists, 17 Belgrave Square, London SW1X 8PG. Tel: 020 7235 2351. Email: rcpsych@rcpsych.ac.uk. Website: www.rcpsych.ac.uk.

RADIOGRAPHER

Diagnostic radiography involves a range of different high-tech methods of examination, including X-rays, computed tomography (CT) scanning, magnetic resonance imaging (MRI) and ultrasound.

Therapeutic radiographers are responsible for targeting the correct dose of radiation at the site of the disease. Working with other specialists, they plan each patient's course of treatment. They also explain the process to the patient and discuss possible side effects and care throughout treatment. During treatment they assess the patient daily, monitor side effects and provide support.

I'm a therapeutic radiographer working with cancer patients. As well as technical skills, you need to be able to attend to the psychological and emotional needs of the patient as well as communicate effectively with other colleagues in the team.

Wendy, Therapeutic Radiographer

Other areas within radiography include radiographer assistants (contact your local NHS employer to see what opportunities are available in your local area), who assist qualified diagnostic and therapeutic radiographers, and imaging support workers who work with radiographers, processing film and assisting patients.

NHS Pay (April 2002)

Helpers	£10,080 – £12,800
Basic (newly qualified)	£17,100 – £19,100
Senior II	£18,300 – £23,400
Senior I and Head IV	£21,800 – £26,000
Head III	£24,900 – £27,600
AHP consultant	£33,900 – £46,600

Usually at least three GCSEs at grade C or above and at least two A levels or equivalent. Some universities have access courses for mature students without the necessary academic qualifications.

Radiography assistant: no formal education or age requirements, although you may need to pass four (or more) GCSEs (or equivalent) to qualify for some more advanced work.

Imaging support worker: there is a relevant NVQ but this is not an entry route to qualification as a radiographer. You may need to pass four (or more) GCSEs (or equivalent) to qualify for some more advanced work.

Further information: Society of Radiographers, 207 Providence Square, Mill Street, London SE1 2EW. Tel: 020 7740 7200. Website: www.sor.org.

ROYAL AIR FORCE MEDICAL CAREERS

DENTAL NURSE

Dental nurses provide a second pair of hands in the surgery. As a dental nurse you will be responsible for looking after all the instruments and equipment in the surgery as well as the smooth running of the surgery itself.

Applicants who wish to be considered for dental hygienist training must possess 5 GCSE/SCEs (Grade C/3) including English language and a science-based subject. The training covers a large part of the National Certificate for Dental Nurses syllabus and you will be encouraged to gain this qualification. Age limits: 17–29.

DENTAL OFFICER

As a newly qualified dentist you'll enter the RAF on a short service commission.

You must be a fully registered and qualified dental practitioner and have GCSE/SCE in English language and maths. Your first year will be spent on a Vocational Training (VT) course while you work in a large practice under a trainer. You'll also do a four-month phase overseas where you will treat service families. After VT you'll have

the opportunity to study for the Diploma in General Dental Practice (DGDP) and possibly the Membership in General Dental Surgery (MGDS). Later, if you have a permanent commission, you may be selected to study for an MSc in a dental discipline or use your postgraduate qualifications as a vocational trainer.
Age limits: 17½–55.

ENVIRONMENTAL HEALTH TECHNICIAN

Environmental health technicians provide professional advice for healthy working and living conditions in all RAF facilities and for service people in all situations.

Minimum qualifications are five GCSEs/SCEs (Grade C/3) including English language, maths, physics (or a physics-based science) and chemistry (or a chemistry-based science). An environmental health technician requires professional qualifications. Age limits: 16–29.

LABORATORY TECHNICIAN

Laboratory technicians work in well-equipped pathology labs in a number of tri-service defence secondary care agency hospital units in the UK and Cyprus, as well as in medical centres on some of the larger RAF stations.

Minimum qualifications are five GCSEs/SCEs (Grade C/3) in English language, maths, biology or human biology, physics and chemistry. Biology, physics or chemistry plus one other subject must be at A/A2 or equivalent. Or you need to be professionally qualified. As a lab technician you are trained in all aspects of pathology before specialising in one of four disciplines: clinical chemistry, haematology, histology or microbiology. If you are an Associate of the Institute of Medical Laboratory Sciences or a Member of the Institute of Biology (Biochemistry or Microbiology), or if you have a science degree relevant to medical lab sciences, you can apply for qualified entry. Age limits: 16–29.

MEDICAL ASSISTANT

The medical support trades provide an essential service to the defence secondary care agency and the RAF at home and overseas. Highly trained staff engage in clinical and medical administrative work at RAF stations, tri-service hospitals, medical units and command headquarters.

You will need to pass a test at Air Force Careers Office (AFCO).
Age limits: 16–29.

MEDICAL OFFICER

The RAF provides modern facilities, back-up and training to help
you develop your GP or specialist skills. It's possible that you could
go on an aeromedical evacuation, where you would provide vital
assistance on search-and-rescue missions, or be involved in
emergency relief flights world-wide.

You will need to be a fully registered medical practitioner or
provisionally registered house officer and have GCSE/SCE in English
language and maths. You can enter as a general duties medical
officer (GDMO) or as a specialist. You'll receive postgraduate training
in your speciality as well as training in aviation medicine. As a GDMO
you'll spend about 18 months in vocational hospital-based training
posts, followed by another 18 months working in a medical centre on
an RAF base approved for GP vocational training. Age limits: house
officer: under 38; fully registered: under 55.

NURSING OFFICER/PSYCHIATRIC NURSE

Princess Mary's Royal Air Force Nursing Service (PMRAFNS) helps
look after the health and fitness of everyone in the RAF. You could
be working in a ward in Cyprus, in a specialist unit in the UK – or
even 30,000 feet up in a Tristar on aeromedical evacuation duties.

You need to be a registered general or mental nurse with two
years' post-registration experience and GCSE/SCE in English
language and maths. You will be encouraged to take courses
pertinent to service needs and to pursue your professional training
in line with post-registration education and practice of the UK
Central Council. Study time is given and paid for by the RAF. Age
limits: 23–38.

RADIOGRAPHER

Radiographers take and process the X-ray images needed for
diagnostic purposes. They work chiefly in the tri-service defence
secondary care agency (DSCA) core hospital at Haslar, the Ministry
of Defence hospital units at Peterborough, Frimley Park or
Derriford, the tri-service rehabilitation unit at Headley Court or
overseas in the Princess Mary's Hospital at RAF Akrotiri in Cyprus.

Minimum qualifications: five GCSEs/SCEs (Grade C/3) including English language, maths and a science. Subjects at A level must total 16 points. Or you need to be professionally qualified. If you already hold a degree or graduate diploma in radiography you'll start your professional work significantly higher in the RAF's rank and pay scales. The RAF also provides training for student radiographers, which has been awarded full accreditation by civilian organisations. Training for an honours degree in diagnostic radiography takes three academic years. Age limits: 18–29.

STAFF NURSE

Nurses in the PMRAFNS provide care for entitled civilians and personnel from other services. They have three main areas of responsibility: primary health care (based on medical centres similar to GP surgeries on RAF stations in the UK and overseas); secondary health care (at one of the Ministry of Defence hospital units at Peterborough, Haslar, Frimley Park or Derriford, in the tri-service rehabilitation unit at Headley Court or overseas in the Princess Mary's Hospital at RAF Akrotiri in Cyprus); and operational roles – assisting in the aeromedical evacuation of casualties from overseas.

You will need to be qualified as a staff nurse (RGN/RMN) (current NMC Registration). Age limits: 21–32.

STUDENT STAFF NURSE

Minimum qualifications: five GCSEs/SCEs (Grade C/3), including English language, maths and a science-based subject. By joining the Princess Mary's Royal Air Force Nursing Service as a student staff nurse you begin your RAF career with nine weeks of recruit training before moving to The University of Central England for your professional nurse training. Age limits: 17 years and 10 months to 32.

Further information: Nursing Services Liaison Team. Tel: 01400 261201 ext. 6782. Email nslo@raf-careers.raf.mod.uk.

ROYAL NAVY MEDICAL CAREERS

MEDICAL OFFICER

The Royal Navy Medical Service (RNMS) comprises 240 medical officers together with about 1,100 nurses, medical assistants (the Navy's paramedics) and medical services officers. Roles in the RNMS are diverse, but its main function is to support the operational navy in war. There are opportunities for research at the Institute of Naval Medicine and elsewhere. All medical officers enter on a six-year Short Career Commission (SCC). Direct entry (qualified) applicants are welcomed. Fifteen undergraduate cadetships are available annually and can be held for a maximum of three years immediately prior to qualification. They are awarded to candidates who pass the Admiralty Interview Board and are subsequently chosen at competitive selection boards.

A doctor in the Royal Navy starts with the new entry medical officers' course (NEMOs), designed to prepare you for your role as a general duties medical officer. Once basic professional training has been completed, and if you opt and are selected for a longer career and specialist registrar, an extended spell of higher specialist training within the NHS and/or Defence Medical Services is usual. The training structure in the services is identical to that in the NHS and subject to the same approval and routine inspection by the Royal Colleges.

MEDICAL ASSISTANT

Medical assistants work alongside medical and dental officers and the Queen Alexandra's Royal Naval Nursing Service (QARNNS). In addition to providing advanced first aid and life saving measures your role will include nursing duties, health education, medical administration and dispensing. You can undertake registered nurse's training with QARNNS. This is open to male ratings as well as to females. If you pass the examinations and are recommended, you will be promoted to leading medical assistant, then petty officer medical assistant and chief petty officer medical assistant. From here, if you have at least two GCSEs (one of which must be English language at Grade C or above) you will be eligible for promotion to warrant officer medical assistant. With a minimum of four GCSEs at Grade C or above (English language and maths are mandatory) you may be recommended for a commission as a medical services officer with the possibility of ultimately reaching the rank of captain.

Following your medical assistant training you could specialise in one of the following:

- General Service Medical Assistant (MA(GS))

- Commando Medical Assistant (MA(CDO))

- Submarine Medical Assistant (MA(SM))

- Medical Assistant – Operating Department Practitioner (MA(ODP))

- Medical Assistant – Dental Surgery Assistant (MA(DSA))

To join the Royal Navy as a medical assistant you need to be aged between 17 and 33. Except for MA (DSA) (for which you require 2 GCSEs including English language and preferably a science or equivalent at Grade C or above) you do not need any special educational qualifications. You will have to pass a selection test, interview and medical examination. The test is based on reasoning, numeracy, literacy and mechanical comprehension. Civilian qualifications considered include:

- City and Guilds of London Institute's certificate in emergency and primary health care

- Health and Safety Executive certificate in first aid at work.

After basic naval training at HMS Raleigh, you spend 12 weeks' intense study at the Defence Medical Services Training Centre (DMSTC), Aldershot. The core subjects are: first aid, environmental and preventive medicine, disorders, advanced first aid, anatomy and physiology, clinical service, administration and pharmacy. You must pass all subjects after each module. Once you have successfully completed this stage of training, you will be awarded the Red Geneva Cross. Part three of your training is 26 weeks spent primarily in a hospital and involves hands-on experience with traumatised and ill patients. This training is backed up with classroom instruction. On completion of part three training, you sit your final examination for medical assistant. You will then be sent to a Sick Bay/Medical Centre in the UK for three months to consolidate what you have learned. On completion of this last stage of your training you will be recognised as a fully trained and qualified medical assistant.

Further information: Royal Navy. Tel: 0845 607 5555.

SCIENTIST IN HAEMOSTASIS AND THROMBOSIS

A modern haematology lab will offer a wide range of tests that monitor the blood coagulation system. Following a detailed clinical examination by a haematologist, blood samples are sent to the lab for testing. Using many different techniques, including recently developed methods in molecular biology, the aim is to identify specific abnormalities in the blood which may upset the delicate balance between factors that promote blood coagulation and those that act as anti-coagulants. As many abnormalities are inherited, it may then be necessary to form extended family studies. Following diagnosis, the lab will also be involved in monitoring the treatment of these patients.

A good degree in one of the biological sciences is the usual entry qualification.

Further information: Recruitment Centre for Clinical Scientists (contact details on p. 30).

SPEECH AND LANGUAGE THERAPIST

Speech and language therapists assess patients and plan individual treatments. Their patients' difficulties could result from many problems, such as learning difficulties, stroke, hearing loss, disorders such as Parkinson's disease or cystic fibrosis, head injuries, cancer, cleft palate or a psychiatric problem. Speech and language therapists work with clients on a one-to-one basis or in groups, perhaps with a physiotherapist or teacher. They are also often involved in educating teachers, parents and carers.

NHS Pay (from 1 April 2001)

Band 1	£15,240–£17,830
Band 2	£18,540–£27,450
Band 3	£30,870–£37,560
Band 4	£36,120–£49,430
Band 5	£37,560–£60,140

Usually five GCSEs, or equivalent, and at least two, usually three, A levels or equivalent are required. Some courses require the passes to be in specific subjects. Some N/SVQs may be alternatives.

I enjoyed the training; it's nice to learn something completely different. Get experience before you apply for training, though, first to see if you like the job and secondly, as competition is so tough, you need to show commitment.

Steph, Speech and Language Therapist

Applications from suitably qualified mature students are welcome. Further information: Royal College of Speech and Language Therapists, 2 White Hart Yard, London SE1 1NX. Tel: 020 7378 1200. Email: postmaster@rcslt.org. Website: www.rcslt.org.

SURGEON

Surgeons specialise in operating on particular parts of the body or to address specific injuries, diseases or degenerative conditions.

CARDIOTHORACIC SURGERY

Cardiothoracic surgery deals with the diagnosis and management of surgical conditions of the heart, lungs and oesophagus. A small aspect of the specialty is the transplantation of both heart and lungs, which is performed in only eight specialised centres in the UK. There are many research opportunities in this specialism and it is expected that trainees will participate in research projects. Consultant cardiothoracic surgeons usually operate about three days per week, have one out-patient clinic and are generally on call one in three or four. In addition there may be a commitment to cardiothoracic transplantation and the care of cardiothoracic trauma.

DENTAL SURGERY
Oral and maxillofacial surgery deals with a variety of conditions associated with the mouth, jaws, face and neck and involves combined medical, dental and surgical training. The work encompasses the management of developmental facial anomalies including cleft lip and palate, facial trauma and surgery required in the management of orofacial malignancy. To become a consultant in oral and maxillofacial surgery you need to be qualified in both medicine and dentistry.

Further information: British Association of Oral and Maxillofacial Surgeons, Royal College of Surgeons of England, 35–43 Lincolns Inn Fields, London WC2A 3PN. Tel: 020 7405 8074. Website: www.baoms.org.uk.

EAR, NOSE AND THROAT SURGERY
Otorhinolaryngology, head and neck surgery, or ENT as it is more popularly known, is a fascinating and diverse specialty. An ENT surgeon may be involved with a neonate's breathing problem, an infant's hearing loss and hearing loss and loss of faculties of old age. Although it is a surgical specialism, it has a very large out-patient medical base. Emergency work is not usually very heavy, although it tends to be dramatic. ENT is ideally suited to flexible working.

GENERAL SURGERY
Ten years ago, general surgery was an integrated specialism consisting of vascular, endocrine, oncological and gastrointestinal work, but it is currently being sub-divided into a set of more clearly defined sub-specialisms, each with its own specialist association. Consultant general surgeons are usually practitioners in one of the areas of vascular, endocrine, oncological and gastrointestinal work.

NEUROSURGERY
Neurosurgery deals with the diagnosis and treatment of pathological processes affecting the nervous system. It includes

the operative, non-operative, intensive care management and rehabilitation of patients with disorders affecting the brain and skull, spine and nervous system. Most consultant neurosurgeons spend four to five sessions in the operating theatre per week with the remainder of the time spent on pre- and post-operative ward care of patients, out-patient clinics, teaching and other administrative duties.

ORTHOPAEDIC AND TRAUMA SURGERY

This is now one of the largest surgical specialisms. A few regional specialist centres for elective surgery remain in this country, but most orthopaedic practice is carried out in a district general hospital along with a general trauma service. Overall there is now a wide range of sub-specialisms within orthopaedic surgery, which allows practitioners to choose interests ranging from microvascular surgery through to major revision arthroplasty of lower limb joints.

PAEDIATRIC SURGERY

Many adult surgical specialties are involved in the surgical care of children, including general surgery, urology, ENT, orthopaedic surgery, ophthalmic surgery, plastic surgery and oral surgery. Such surgery is usually undertaken in district general hospitals. The surgeons involved deal mostly with adult patients and may not have received much specialised paediatric training. Specialist paediatric surgery includes: neonatal surgery (mostly the surgery of congenital abnormalities); major intestinal surgery of infants and children; major trauma surgery; children's cancer surgery and paediatric urology. In addition, non-specialist paediatric surgery may include the management of minor common problems such as hernia, circumcision, undescended testis etc.

PLASTIC SURGERY

This covers a wide field of reconstructive and reparative surgery, both in its own right and also in combination with many other surgical and medical sub-specialisms. Basic scientific and clinical research is encouraged and trainee surgeons with inquiring minds will find a wealth of potential research projects within the field of plastic and reconstructive surgery. Since few procedures in plastic surgery are identical, the work is stimulating, challenging, exciting and encourages innovation. There is a strong nine-to-five component but also a challenging amount of out-of-hours work, mostly involving the management of burns injury and the treatment of severe facial, hand and lower limb injuries.

Those wishing to follow a typical surgical career path begin basic surgical training as a senior house officer and go on to pass the Member of the Royal College of Surgeons (MRCS) examination. Basic training takes a minimum of two years in posts approved by the college for their training and educational content. On completion of basic surgical training a trainee then seeks a post at the higher surgical training level in one of nine surgical specialisms: cardiothoracic, general, neurological, oral and maxillofacial, orthopaedic, otolaryngology, paediatric, plastic, urology. This period of training is done at the specialist registrar grade where trainees expand their clinical experience, take on increasing responsibilities and develop a specialist interest. Higher training takes five or six years, depending on the specialism, and after four years a trainee is eligible to take the intercollegiate examination. This leads to the award of the FRCS diploma. Once all training is completed, the required examinations passed and the CCST (Certificate of Completion of Specialist Training) gained, the qualified surgeon can then enter the General Medical Council's (GMC's) Specialist Register and apply for a post as a consultant. Continuing professional development (CPD) is an essential part of the consultant's work, including learning new skills, taking and teaching courses, giving lectures, carrying out research and developing new techniques.

Further information: Royal College of Surgeons of England, 25–43 Lincolns Inn Fields, London WC2A 3PN. Tel: 020 7405 3474. Website: www.rcseng.ac.uk.

USEFUL CONTACTS

BRITISH PSYCHOLOGICAL SOCIETY
St Andrew's House, 48 Princess Road East, Leicester LE1 7DR. Tel: 0116 254 9568. Email: mail@bps.org.uk. Website: www.bps.org.uk.

NHS CAREERS
The NHS and education sector welcomes people with alternative

academic and vocational qualifications. NHS Careers Helpline: 0845 606 0655. Email: advice@nhscareers.nhs.uk. The NHS pays all tuition fees at diploma and degree level: overseas applicants will be subject to current residential requirements. For further information contact NHS Students Grant Unit on 01253 856123.

NURSING AND MIDWIFERY ADMISSIONS SERVICE (NMAS)

Rosehill, New Barn Lane, Cheltenham, Gloucestershire GL52 3LZ. Tel: 01242 544949 (general enquiries); 01242 223707 (application materials). Website: www.nmas.ac.uk.

UNIVERSITIES AND COLLEGES ADMISSION SERVICE (UCAS)

PO Box 28, Cheltenham, Gloucestershire, GL50 3SH. Website: www.ucas.ac.uk.

CHAPTER 5

What Next?

If you've read through the book to this last chapter, you must have found something of interest in it. You're still hooked on the idea of a career in medicine – or you might not have been hooked to start with, but you're getting hooked now! Your confidence has increased because you realise that you do have the basic qualitities and some of the transferable skills to make a success of medicine. You've cast your eye over the plethora of career opportunities and one or two have grabbed your attention. You understand the basics of what you need in order to qualify. So what now?

For most careers in medicine, you need to be committed. Firstly for the training – quite a chunk of your life will be spent in study and training. Can you hack it? Can you dedicate the time to what might be long-term study? How do you feel about studying? If you feel your study skills aren't up to much, you can always learn how to improve them. Don't let this barrier hold you back.

Can you afford to study? Some courses are part-time, so maybe you could work part-time. Or you might prefer full-time study. How are you going to fund yourself? Here are some routes you might like to explore with regard to financial assistance with training:

- Career Development Loan. These loans are made to cover the cost of fees, books, materials and living costs for 24 months. Applicants need to be 18 years or older and intending to participate in a job-related course. Tel: 0800 585505. Website: www.lifelonglearning.co.uk/cdl/index.

- Citizens Advice Bureau. They have a database of local charities and trusts, which may be able to provide grants for students.

- DfES Student Support. Website: www.dfes.gov.uk. This website is for students living in England and Wales who want to know what financial help is available to them as higher education students.

- Educational Grants Advisory Service (EGAS). Provides information on charitable institutions that may be able to assist students. Tel: 020 7249 6636.

- Local Education Authorities. You should contact your local education for their position on mandatory awards.

- Student Loans Company Ltd. Information on loans for higher education students in the UK. Website: www.slc.co.uk.

So you've got the commitment and the funding sussed. What about career prospects? Other than practising your health discipline in a variety of settings, e.g. private and public, you could:

- become involved in integrated healthcare (complementary and conventional)

- set up your own clinic

- teach your discipline

- write about it

- sell products related to it

- take your discipline abroad

- set up your own training establishment

- have your own website

- become involved in research.

But what do you *do* next? You could:

- contact any of the institutions/organisations mentioned in this book related to your areas of interest

- contact your local further education college or higher education institution to see what health-related courses they offer

- contact Learn Direct, the national learning advice organisation, where you can find out how to improve your skills with one of 750 specially designed courses, search the database of 500,000 nationwide courses, access practical information and advice on learning or explore ways of using work-based learning to gain university qualifications. Tel: 0800 100900. Website: www.learndirect.co.uk.

- visit your local library to find out more about careers in medicine

- read these publications:

  Getting into Psychology, John Handley
  Getting into Physiotherapy, Laurel Alexander
  Getting into Healthcare Professions, Laurel Alexander
  Getting into Nursing and Midwifery, Janet Higgins
  Getting into Medical School, Jim Burnett and Joe Ruston

  So you want to be a Doctor? David Hopkins
  Insider's Guide to Medical Schools 2003–2004, edited by Ian Urmston, Liz Corps and Kristian Mears
  Careers in Nursing and Related Professions, Linda Nazarko
  Careers in Medicine, Dentistry and Mental Health, Judith Humphreys and Loulou Brown

So this is it. The end of the book. But possibly the beginning of an exciting and rewarding new career in medicine for you. Good luck!

END PIECE

The Evolution of Medicine
I have an earache . . .
2000 BC – Here, eat this root.
1000 AD – That root is heathen. Here, say this prayer.
1850 AD – That prayer is superstition. Here, drink this
potion.
1940 AD – That potion is snake oil. Here, swallow this pill.
1985 AD – That pill is ineffective. Here, take this antibiotic.
2000 AD – That antibiotic is artificial. Here, eat this root.